REFORM
JUDAISM TODAY

Book Two
WHAT WE BELIEVE

Book Two

WHAT
WE
BELIEVE

REFORM JUDAISM TODAY

Eugene B. Borowitz

BEHRMAN HOUSE, INC. New York

Library of Congress Cataloging in Publication Data

Borowitz, Eugene B.
  Reform Judaism Today.

  CONTENTS: Book 1. Reform in the process of
change. Book 2. What we believe. Book 3. How we
live.
  1. Central Conference of American Rabbis. Reform
Judaism, a centenary perspective. 2. Reform
Judaism—United States. I. Title.
BM197.B67   296.8'346   77-24676
ISBN O-87441-271-4 (v. 1)

© Copyright 1977 by Eugene B. Borowitz
Published by Behrman House, Inc.
1261 Broadway, New York, New York 10001

Produced in the U.S. of America

CONTENTS

REFORM
JUDAISM TODAY

Book Two
WHAT WE BELIEVE

PART I

An Introduction to the Principles

The paragraph on God in *Reform Judaism: A Centenary Perspective* opens the major portion of the statement, consisting of six numbered paragraphs, that rather naturally falls into two sections. Each of the headings in the latter section, paragraphs IV-VI, begins "Our Obligations," a theme examined here in terms of three contemporary concerns: religious duties, the State of Israel and the Diaspora, and service to the Jewish people and to humanity at large. The headings for paragraphs I-III, however, do not include such a phrase in common. Rabbi Jack Stern, Jr. pointed out in one of the last meetings of the committee drafting the *Centenary Perspective* that these paragraphs also have a common focus. He called them the "principles" of the statement, since they treat of God, the Jewish people, and Torah, and these constitute the basic beliefs of the Jewish community. There is, then, a nice balance to the substantive section of the document, with three paragraphs on principles balanced by three paragraphs on obligations. The symmetry was not consciously intended by those who worked on or contributed to the shaping of the document. It was, however, a most congenial result of the drafting process, since it seemed to the committee to give balanced expression to their sense of Reform Judaism. Yet it was decided not to use a thematic title for these first three paragraphs. The terms *principles* and *beliefs* seemed rather grandiose, perhaps even somewhat dogmatic, and the committee preferred to avoid making such authoritative claims for their work.

The sense of proper balance was further borne out by the discrepancy in size between the exposition of the beliefs and that of the duties. The first three paragraphs are each much shorter than each of the last three. One might expect a religious document to stress theological principles, especially in so complicated a time as ours when belief does not come or stay easily. But historically that has not been true of Judaism. Our religion has always emphasized our duties more than any philosophy which might serve as their basis. This traditional Jewish concern with action more than creed is reflected here and is explicitly referred to at the beginning of the section on obligations, paragraph IV, on religious practice (on which, see chapters 12 to 15). This stress on what Jews should be doing was a conscious response to what seems the major interest of concerned Jews in our time. There is some spiritual search in our community, and a good deal more questioning about Jewish identity—that is, just what being a Jew means today. Most Jews, however, express their Jewish intent in a rather Jewish way, by asking what they should do. So books like *The Jewish Catalog* or the Central Conference of American Rabbis' *Shabbat Manual* are very much more in demand than books on Jewish theology. Since the *Centenary Perspective* is directed to a given moment—the centenaries of the Union of American Hebrew Congregations and the Hebrew Union College-Jewish Institute of Religion—it speaks to the present situation, seeking to respond directly to its needs.

It should also be pointed out that these hundred years of nationally organized Reform Judaism have yielded a certain measure of agreement in the area of beliefs. Or, to put it more precisely, we have arrived at a good working consensus as to what we hold in common and what we can reasonably (though not always comfortably!) leave to personal decision. Through the many months in which hundreds of people commented on the various drafts of the document there were no major philosophic differences over what the text said or did not say. The overwhelming majority of Reform Rabbis—and, I suggest, Conservative Rabbis and American Jews generally—shares a common sense of modern Jewish belief. This commonality is quite limited in its content, to be sure, and it most certainly allows for variety and development in Jewish faith in ways that go far beyond what our tradition knew or, more certainly, ever put in explicit form. The brevity of these first three paragraphs reflects the consolidation of that consensus; most fortunately, the committee was able to put it into words early in its work. Had it tried to say very much more, it would have passed into the realm of controversy. Knowing what is to be left to individual opinion is also a major part of reaching social agreement.

There was an additional reason for being brief about matters of basic Jewish belief. In this sort of format one cannot hope to say very much to begin with. Would expanding the section on God from five sentences to eight or even twenty suffice to make a major difference in answering our questions about God? Further, saying more, not being brief almost to the point of terseness, might make it seem as if enough *had* been said, that this was somehow as much as most people needed to know. By keeping these paragraphs as short as they reasonably could be, the committee tried to signal the reader that they are but a bare introduction to the most important matters of Jewish faith. Their very form calls for more study and investigation. Having said only about as much as one can say to someone standing on one foot, they carry with them Hillel's legendary closing dictum—is it not also part of his concise description of Torah?—"Go study!"

PART II

God

The affirmation of God has always been essential to our people's will to survive. In our struggle through the centuries to preserve our faith we have experienced and conceived of God in many ways. The trials of our own time and the challenges of modern culture have made steady belief and clear understanding difficult for some. Nevertheless, we ground our lives, personally and communally, on God's reality and remain open to new experiences and conceptions of the Divine. Amid the mystery we call life, we affirm that human beings, created in God's image, share in God's eternality despite the mystery we call death.

I.
God

From the Centenary Perspective

CHAPTER ONE

Jewish Survival and Our Sense of God

RELYING ON INTUITION

When people do talk about belief in God in our time they tend to do so in personal terms, often quite personal, referring to their innermost feelings and the like. In part that has to do with the Protestant influence on our culture. Against the authority of the Catholic Church, Luther emphasized what individuals knew to be true as God gave them, personally, the truth. Over the centuries, particularly in the United States, this Protestant teaching has become associated with the notion of conversion as "seeing the light" and with the phenomenon of revival movements. This way of being religious, with its emphasis on the emotions and the change effected on one's personality, has generally been uncongenial to Jews. Conversion in Judaism is a matter of education and will, not the result of a special gift of God. Besides, most Jews are born into the Jewish relationship with God. They may know moments of great personal intimacy with God—the Psalms show how far back this goes in our tradition—but what goes on *inside* the

Jew is not the major focus of the Jew's religious life.

For cultural and philosophical reasons, too, Jews have been uncomfortable with the stress on subjectivity. Being so much a part of big-city, secular life, they find it bringing God too much into the foreground of existence. Being largely university-trained and intellectually oriented, they are skeptical of religious claims that seem so much based on emotion and so little attuned to reason. Nonetheless, when modern Jews have talked about God, they too have done so in personal terms—though, I hasten to add, these have generally been philosophical. The individual or individual experience has been the starting point of most modern Jewish religious thought. The most common way of pointing to God has been to refer to the person's conscience, to insist that its mandates derive from something greater than what we have been taught by our families or our society, that its ultimate source is God. More rigorous intellectual arguments work from the order we intuit in a highly complex universe, or the way our search for all-embracing ideas is the summit of all our thinking, and the testimony that behind all things is the God who is One. Or, beginning with the feeling aspects of being human, we describe our awe that anything exists, our wonder that existence is so grand and thus our sensitivity to God who is its ground. We then regularly use interesting verbs to describe our faith: we "sense," or "feel," or "know" there is a God, all in ways that we do not commonly use these verbs (and thus my quotation marks). In each case the way to God, whether more rational or more intuitive, is personal and inner.

UNDERSTANDING OURSELVES THROUGH OUR BELIEFS

There is good reason for modern Jewish thinkers to follow this line of thought while recognizing its possible Protestant background. In the late eighteenth century a crisis developed in humanity's thinking about religion—about science, too, I should add. Previously people had little difficulty believing that if we could think about the world quite clearly in our minds, then we could be fairly certain of what the world itself was. The crisis came when it was pointed out, in ways which have been practically impossible to ignore ever since, that what we think about the world might say more about us and the way we think than it says about the world. For religion that meant that our ideas about God—more specifically, our proofs that God was "out there,"—also said more about us than about reality. Since then, reasoning about religion has had to start with what we know about ourselves, how we think or what we experience, our ethical or esthetic sense. Whatever certainty we can have must start with us. Such belief as we will affirm must

first convince us personally. We feel we not
only have the right to question those who
come to us asking us to believe things, but that
we have a duty to do so if we are to be true to
ourselves, the one thing we really have and
know. Skepticism is part of our modern sensibility; it is thus a necessary part of modern
believing. We have faith and question it,
moving on thereby to deeper, clearer faith and
to more searching questions. Our sort of believing cannot for long stand still. So all modern
religious thought, general and Jewish, focuses
upon the individual, working from the individual to God, or, for traditionalists, showing
how the individual is fulfilled by God's
revelation.

THE SCOPE OF PERSONAL AUTONOMY

Individualism has been fundamental to Reform
Judaism. The earliest Reform Jews thought
mostly in terms of the rights of their generation as against those of the tradition. Specifically they felt they were as entitled to define
what a Jewish life meant in their radically
changed social situation, as previous generations had been in their time and place.
Gradually this became the right of individual
Reform Jews to determine for themselves what
they would believe and, more importantly,
what they would do, continuing the tradition
or creating new patterns of Jewish life. The
century of Reform Jewish history which the

Centenary Perspective has in view cannot be understood without this growing emphasis on individualism, what contemporary writers often term personal autonomy. The first historical paragraph of the *Centenary Perspective* mentions this as one of the things that Reform Judaism has taught many modern Jews, that "Jewish obligation begins with the informed will of every individual." This is the basis for the diversity in Reform Judaism, discussed in the last of the historical paragraphs of the *Centenary Perspective*, and it shapes the special problems and opportunities involved in defining the Reform Jew's religious duties (section IV, paragraph III). Giving such power to the individual is the basis of Reform Judaism's difference not only from Orthodoxy but from much of Conservative Judaism as well.

In Orthodoxy, what God has made known in the Torah and the Torah tradition is more important than what the individual comes to believe is true—or, to put it more precisely, the complete fulfillment of one's individuality as a Jew is to be found in the Torah as given by God and interpreted by our modern sages. In Conservative Judaism the individual mind and conscience may be granted greater influence, but individuals should not define Jewish observance for themselves but should, as in the past, follow the leadership given a modern, observant community through an official body of its scholars. Reform Jews, agreeing that the Torah tradition provides invaluable guidance and that scholars are uniquely equipped to discern the lessons of the past, nonetheless emphasize the right of individual Jews to make the final decision as to what constitutes Jewish belief and practice for them. The Reform respect for personal autonomy carries that far.

JEWISH IDENTITY AND
JEWISH SURVIVAL

Yet this distinctive Reform Jewish emphasis on individualism is absent from the opening of this paragraph on God. Mostly that is because it can be taken for granted. Years of Reform Jewish teaching about thinking for oneself may be counted on as the background readers will bring to this statement. Since it is concise and directed to the immediate, centenary situation of Reform Judaism, it concentrates on the relation of the Jewish people's age-old will to survive and its affirmation of God. The emphasis is communal, not individual, for this has been the special concern of recent years. The Holocaust, the accomplishments of the State of Israel, and, more dramatically, the threats to Israel's existence have made most American Jews realize how much their precious individuality is tied to the Jewish people. And Jewish identity has again largely become a question of Jewish survival, whether that of the State of Israel, of Jews in the Soviet Union or other oppressive countries, or of Jewish life in the United States darkly threatened by apathy, ignorance, and intermarriage. Even as individualism highlighted Reform Judaism's development through much of this past century, so the responsibilities and hopes of Jewish peoplehood have since the 1950s and '60s come to the fore of Reform Jewish consciousness. As the second historical paragraph notes, Reform Jews have learned from recent history "new heights of aspiration and devotion" to the Jewish people and that its survival . . . is of highest priority."

Paradoxical as it may seem, we see in this survival of the Jews despite everything an indication that God is real. That the Jews have endured these many centuries in dignity and service; that they continue to be a living presence in history while many of their oppressors have effectively died; that they have refused to stop being Jews and linking their lives with the Torah despite prejudice and persecution; that in the face of the unprecedented tragedies of our time they remain humanly undefeated and Jewishly determined; that regardless of their widespread and manifest faithlessness they remain recognizably loyal to the Jewish tradition and its messianic outlook—all this is not mere biological urge, historical quirk, or sociological oddity. Jewish existence reflects something far transcending itself. We are skeptics, yet we know Jewish history says something about God. We do not believe much, but in the presence of the indomitable Jewish will to be and be Jewish, we sense God's power. We care about the Jews because— quietly, to be sure—we care about God. When we worry about the Jews and their future we naturally wonder where God is and why God doesn't do more to help us. This is not some childish remnant in our psyche, merely an infantile hope that Daddy/Mommy will save us. It is our deep, bedrock sense that, odd as it may sound to say it so plainly, the Jews are involved with God. And the *Centenary Perspective* points to the fact that in our time we gain a special sense of God's reality by our intimate involvement with the Jews.

SEEING GOD'S ROLE IN JEWISH SURVIVAL

More, *The Perspective* says that Jews have always known that their existence had more than tribal worth. So they took courage from knowing that their struggle to exist and to do so in decency was substantially for God's sake. And they hoped that as they put forth their effort so God would, in the mysterious ways that God affects human affairs, help them. Many individual Jews and Jewish communities were lost in the process. The Jewish people has survived. In inexplicably roundabout ways God's protection has manifested itself. We today are far less likely to await God's active providence. Yet we also believe that as we work for our people, we work for what is most precious and significant in the universe and draw its power to ourselves.

Here, as in so much of the *Centenary Perspective*, a balance is struck between two themes, in this case devotion to God and devotion to our people. Seeing diverse aspects of our faith in relation to one another keeps them from being taken in isolation and thus extended to unfortunate extremes. Thus to concentrate one's Jewishness so fully on belief in God that one has no room left in one's heart or will for the Jewish people strikes us as so self-centered an individualism as hardly worthy of consideration for the title *Judaism*. Yet, similarly, to be so devoted to the survival of the Jewish people as to forget that there is a God and that this people takes its significance from its relationship with God seems an odd way for the people of the Torah to hope to have a future—though considering the threats to the Jewish people in our time errors on this side of the spectrum are easy to understand and forgive.

THE PHILOSOPHICAL PROBLEM

Incidentally, this contemporary Jewish concern with corporate identity sets a special problem before modern Jewish philosophers. Thinkers of a previous generation clarified the individual aspects of being a Jew. Much of their teaching remains valid and is indispensable to any future philosophy of Judaism. It is, as noted above, the accepted background for all the topics treated in the *Centenary Perspective*. But now the problem arises, how can we balance their individualism with our sense of equally being members of a people? Can we find a way to describe our intuition that Jewish history testifies to God's reality which will be as convincing as the ways preceding philosophers moved from individual experience to God? The problems are formidable, particularly as modern philosophy gives almost no credence to group experience or group authority. The *Perspective* therefore leaves this matter, as so many others, to the scholars and their deliberations.

CHAPTER TWO

The Different Ways of Knowing God

FAITH AND DOUBT

There is a tendency to think that Jews of other eras had unfaltering faith and never were troubled by doubts about God. Mostly that is romantic nonsense. There is hardly a major Jewish book in which problems of belief do not come to the fore. Philosophers like Saadia and Maimonides write in the introductions to their works that they were prompted to set down their ideas because Jews in their time were so confused and doubting.

The major difference between previous ages and ours is that once most people and cultures were religious. Today religion is on the defensive in intellectual circles, and faith seems more the exception than the rule. Yet, while understanding God is particularly difficult in our secular time, it has always been something of a problem. Our questioning is not utterly unprecedented and thus not thoroughly un-Jewish. If anything—and this is the reflection of our modern view of life and history—we cannot imagine that any great idea could stay alive and meaningful if it had not been subject to doubt

19

and change. Jews lived among many religious groups: idolaters, Zoroastrians, Christians, Muslims. They lived in many climates, cultures, societies, economies, governments. It is inconceivable to us that they were never influenced by these experiences, that their basic ideas always remained the same. Were someone able to show such stability over several thousand years we would immediately guess that what survived had very little validity.

A DYNAMIC SENSE OF TRUTH

Premodern people did not look at change this way. They thought permanence was the mark of truth. Something that was true never changed, or never did so in any significant way. We still retain something of that sense. If truth changes, that implies there must be several truths, which seems a contradiction in terms. Jewish faith would say that, as there is one God, there is ultimately only one truth. The problem we face, however, is whether anybody but God can know it—the one, whole truth. Even if the premoderns didn't think they knew it all, they thought they knew much of it. We are more modest. We think the most we can claim is that we are growing toward such comprehensive understanding—though every once in a while it looks as if what we thought was a better sense of truth turns out to be a lot less than that. Our sense of truth is dynamic, moving, and we do not see why, whether previous generations were conscious of it or not, it should not have been that way in the past.

A major revolution took place when this notion of truth-as-growing—that is, of change—came into our understanding of Judaism. For if Judaism had changed in the past, then there was no reason why it could not change in the present. More, if change was the means to Jewish survival, then those who refused to change Judaism were dooming the Jewish people. There is, then, a moral, divine impera-tive to change when it is needed to meet the exigencies of the time. This was the intuition which sustained the Reform Jews of the early nineteenth century. They knew that a western-ized, participating Jewry could not merely adapt a few of the patterns and practices of a Jewry that had been segregated for centuries. They knew some major changes were required, and boldly they set out to make them. In the arguments which ensued they proved that this was what had been done in Judaism in the past. They created the "Science of Judaism"—our poor translation of an important German term—*Wissenschaft des Judentum*—by rigor-ously applying the notion of change to the history of their people. In the hands of an early Reform Jewish master like Abraham Geiger the idea so illuminated the past records of the Jewish people that, as the opening paragraphs of the *Centenary Perspective* testify, its place in Judaism has by now been accepted by almost all Jews.

The Jewish sense of God has been no exception to this rule. Some things seem to have remained relatively stable. Chief of these is the notion that God is one. Yet scholars have pointed to places in the Bible where it seems as if God rules only over the Land of Israel, implying that there are other gods elsewhere. Another supposition has it that there were other divine beings, though these did not reach God's status. Another stable feature would seem to be God's own name, which we regularly do not pronounce, substituting instead *Adonai,* "My Lord." Yet almost everyone knows that there are other names for God in the Bible and that the rabbis and the mystics invented other titles by which to call God. As we now study the record of the way Jews historically have talked about God it seems quite clear that time and temperament, culture and personality have always had a part in shaping Jewish views of God.

EXPERIENCE AND CONCEPTION

The *Centenary Perspective* points to both what we have "experienced" and what we have "conceived" of God. The difference between them is important enough to merit some attention. Experience covers a great range of what people go through. What they conceive is limited to that to which they give intellectual form and expression, generally their concepts and ideas. For a religion as sophisticated and intellectual as Judaism, conceiving of God can be quite important. Yet most people find such abstraction beyond them. They believe in God and, insofar as that is based on something in their lives (or the life of their people, like the giving of the Law at Sinai), we say they have experienced God. It once would have seemed self-evident that some sort of religious experience is part of most people's lives, but contemporary society is quite stringent in getting us to repress our sense of the sacred. Nonetheless, many people can remember occasions when God was real to them. But few people are theologians. They do not try to create a pattern of ideas which will adequately explain what they have felt. Somewhere between the many who experience and the elite who philosophize are the poets and storytellers who put their sense of God into words that very many people can respond to and be inspired by. We are more likely to recognize God as a Process than as a Shepherd, yet there is something in that ancient way of depicting God that still moves us, and it is not clear how many of our modern terms for God will survive for centuries, not to ask about millennia. Modern Jews of whatever personal bent can be grateful for the extraordinary variety of the Jewish effort to get close to God, for it gives them courage in their own quest and guidance in making their own formulations.

Reform Jews of an earlier period were somewhat less open than this to the diversity of Jewish relationships with God. They thought of Judaism, and certainly of Reform Judaism, as a rational religion. By this they meant, at least, that modern people, wanting to think for themselves and accepting only what they felt was believable, would find Reform Judaism's appeal to the mind more than to tradition particularly appealing. They also believed that Judaism addressed itself essentially to the intellect—in which they included the moral and esthetic senses—and that its chief contribution to humanity was its way of thinking about God, what they called Judaism's God-idea or concept of God. One can give good reasons for their taking this position. In their day it was critical to demonstrate that superstition and magic were not essential to Jewish belief and practice, that the fundamental truth of Judaism was equal to and compatible with the best of modern science and philosophy. Their emphasis on ethics as a chief manifestation of Jewish piety and their demonstration that Jews share in the universal concerns and responsibilities of humankind were crucial to generations of Jews emerging from ghetto segregation, and they remain important teachings today.

Yet identifying Reform Judaism so closely with rationality also caused problems. If our religion is mainly a matter of the mind, then what happens to our heart and its devotion, to the prayer, the ritual, the simple human trust that once were such important parts of Jewish piety? As people are more than rational beings, so religion is rightly more than an intellectual affair. This critique is less than fair to those early Reform Jews who courageously pioneered the new forms of being Jewish from which we all still derive. These rationalists, it should be remembered, fostered the development of modern Jewish music and liturgies. They were not so narrowly philosophical as to refuse to speak to the heart. Yet they were very much more concerned with conceiving of God rather than with experiencing God. With God essentially an idea, later Reform Jews found their practice of Judaism somewhat cold and unmoving. The present generation, while not denying the validity or value of the intellectual approach to God, recognizes that Judaism has been and today should be equally hospitable to those whose relation to God is of that more personal, inexpressible, varied sort we call experience.

CHAPTER THREE

The Special Problems
of Belief in Our Time

Though Jews have always had something of a problem finding or conceptualizing God, we can identify two special sources of difficulty in this regard in our time: the events of history and the challenges of culture. As recently as the late 1950s the religious literature of the Jewish community would have emphasized the latter rather than the former.

HISTORY AS AFFECTIVE EXPERIENCE

When we speak of the trials of history now, our minds immediately move to the Holocaust and to the traumas in the United States and the world of the early 1970s. Yet the Holocaust did not emerge as a major Jewish religious issue until the mid-1960s. No one is quite sure why. The facts were known in 1945 as the war in Europe came to an end, and in the next year or two pictures and documents regularly circulated in the American Jewish community. They had some effect upon us, yet there is no equivalent in the literature of that time to the debate concerning the "meaning" of the Holocaust which took place twenty years later. The easiest explanations are psychological. The pain was too great and we wanted to forget it. We felt so guilty at having survived, even at a distance, or at having done so little, although almost all American Jews knew nothing of what was going on, that we wanted to forget what had happened. Or, more positively, we channeled our feelings into doing things for the survivors. There were European refugees to care for, a State of Israel to be founded and then supported, immigrants to the United States to help. We were caught up in America's gigantic social relocation, its economic expansion and consequent rush to suburbia which plunged us into forming new Jewish communities and building new Jewish institutions. Was there something about the civil rights movement of the early '60s that roused us to what had happened when good people in Germany stood idly by? Or was it the capture and trial of Eichmann? Or the development of a Christian death-of-God movement which made it socially acceptable for American Jews to raise doubts about God? Or were we finally secure enough in our Jewishness and Americanism to raise such questions? The answers are by no means clear. Until the mid-1960s, however, it was culture, not history, which disturbed Jewish belief most.

THE CHALLENGES OF CULTURE

The challenge had come first from the triumphs

of science. Through the post-World War II period there were many American Jews who felt that the Jewish sense of God needed radical reconstruction in terms of what science said about reality. They worried about the Genesis story of creation as against current astronomical speculations and the theory of evolution; about the miracles of the Bible as against the scientific implausibility of such stories; and about the biblical images of God as having a face, an arm, or emotions. The standard liberal response was to invoke the idea of change. The Bible spoke in its language and we would speak in ours. Some of the Bible was "myth," a symbolic story, in which one used everyday events to describe a reality beyond the human—and so the stories of the Creation, Adam and Eve, and the Flood. Thus the facts of these tales may be faulted, but we cannot complain about the sense of ultimate reality contained in them. The miracles, too, seemed easily explicable as the exaggerated way people would tell of great events, particularly when they believed God had helped them at critical moments in history. And the Bible's anthropomorphic portrayals of God could be seen as an early and still appealing symbolism. This liberal way of reading the problem passages of the Bible became rather widely accepted among American Jewry. Nonetheless, to this day there are people who emerge from their religious education—or the lack of it—and are shocked when they try to take some of the passages of the Bible or prayerbook literally. This continuing experience has prompted some American Jewish thinkers to call for a thoroughly revised way of speaking about God. They suggest talking of divinity in thoroughly scientific terms, most usually in terms of the ordering process in nature.

Similar problems arose from other aspects of culture. Psychoanalysis reduced all inner experience of God to wish fulfillment or the projection of father/mother into the universe to love/judge us, depending on our psychic needs. Sociology and anthropology came along to show us how many of the ideas and practices we had thought unique in Judaism were paralleled in other cultures and were therefore best explained as human needs rather than God's commands. The Marxians insisted that religion was fundamentally a means with which the upper classes keep the lower classes from rebelling, and exposed Judaism as more concerned with maintaining the etiquette of the newly arrived upper-middle class than with serving God with any seriousness. In general, the vibrant, exciting cultural activities of our time were secular—that is, they were nonreligious, when they were not antireligious. This modern culture made religious faith seem primitive or regressive. For all Reform Judaism's efforts to show that one could be fully modern and Jewish at the same time, for all its philosophical expertise, its moral passion, and its esthetic concerns, belief remained an odd way for a serious person to face reality.

QUESTIONS RAISED BY HISTORY AND CULTURE

Something of these challenges still remains in the Jewish community, but it does not seem to have the force today that it once had. I am convinced that the reason for this emphasis is a major shift in our center of confidence. Once we knew that whatever the university, the bestseller, the important magazine told us was true. Judaism would have to adjust to it—though it never managed to catch up. As long as we put our trust in high culture, we had doubts about Judaism. Only we have increasingly begun to doubt culture. We have been shocked by a science which wanted to know about things but set aside questions of right and wrong, by a technology which used science for profit yet at great human cost, by a psychiatry which rarely cured, by writers and artists who exposed but could not exalt the human condition. Jews remain disproportionately involved in all American cultural activities. They do not, as they once did, seem to make it their substitute for religion. As culture has become only important but no longer our major source of truth, its challenge to religion, while real, has tended to decline.

By contrast, we have been more shaken by

what we have seen happen in human history. Permit me, for a moment, to defer comment on the Holocaust and speak instead of more recent events. We can hardly believe what we have seen, again and again, revealed about human nature. The Watergate exposures were only a part of a whole series of disillusionments. The Vietnam War taught us America could be as stupid and self-righteous as any other nation, that its leaders would sacrifice lives and an economy rather than admit their errors, that though the calamity was evident to the overwhelming majority of Americans, the bloodshed was prolonged. Assassination and riot; pious preaching about civil rights, wars on poverty, aid to the powerless, while all remained the same; corruption in business; FBI and CIA illegalities; benign recessions; muggings and rapes; cynicism and self-serving; a society was going pagan. Internationally, the same tragedy was played on a larger, distant stage. No community had put more faith in the United Nations than did the Jews. We thought it would bring reason and justice into international affairs. We dreamed of peace, perhaps even of a more equitable world economic order where nations would begin to live out the common humanity of people. Instead we got Yasir Arafat appearing with gun in holster and the denunciation of the State of Israel for rescuing its citizens from Uganda but not of the terrorists who seized them or the government which abetted the terrorists.

In such a time it has been difficult to believe in anything—reason, morality, people, God. Almost all the institutions in which we placed our trust, the very human nature on which we counted eventually to bring justice into the world—these have betrayed us. They have turned out to be unworthy of the confidence we placed in them. What sort of God would create, or order, or abide, or not do something about such a world? If God is good, then why do such terrible things regularly happen and why does not God work for the good?

This is the same range of questions which are raised by the Holocaust. I thought it best to mention the contemporary issues first because I wanted to make certain that we did not consider the Holocaust merely a historical or parochial matter, one significant only for another time or only to one people. I do not deny these particular elements in it, but what happened to European Jewry in World War II forecast something of how the following decades have assaulted the entire human community. What the Nazis showed us about the possibilities of human behavior has been repeated in smaller and less stupefying ways, yet ones which reflect a similar decadence if not depravity. The *Centenary Perspective* does not specifically mention the Holocaust in speaking of history's challenge to faith in God. It seemed wiser to recognize how many other events have deeply troubled us and to link the

Holocaust with them as part of our continuing trial.

The *Perspective* also notes that not everyone was moved to skepticism. "The trials of our time and the challenges of modern culture have made steady belief and clear understanding difficult *for some*" [italics mine]. Those whose belief or understanding of Judaism was deeply shaken attracted much community attention with their dramatic protest against the tradition and their search for a new way of facing reality. For many others the difficulties were much more modest. "Steady" faith gave way to moments of doubt which often enough were then followed by fresh belief. The "clear" understandings of a previous day gave way to confusion and not infrequently moved on to new and more satisfactory conceptions of God. For such people we cannot speak of a loss of belief, only of a time of insecurity and fluctuation in faith, one which sometimes was as much a period of growth as it was of pain. And for a small minority none of this mattered. Somehow their faith was never touched. They knew what was happening around them, and to them, and yet they believed. Eliezer Berkovits has called our attention to the fact that many people who went through the Holocaust never raised the questions that some people who were far from it popularized. He argues that we should be less concerned to follow the doubters, a common human category in this secular time, than to keep faith with the believers, an uncommon group in any time, but one which, considering the circumstances of their steadfastness, is worthy of our awe and emulation. I myself have always marveled that Leo Baeck, the great Liberal rabbi of Berlin, the only major modern Jewish thinker to have spent the war in a concentration camp, emerged from his experience without the need to question or revise what he had written about Jewish faith many happy years earlier.

CHAPTER FOUR

Responding to the Challenges

UNANSWERED QUESTIONS

Having described our difficult situation, the *Centenary Perspective* then responds to it in only one word, "Nevertheless." This is not an answer, at least in the intellectual sense. A number of people have tried to give such answers. Some have suggested that God must be thought of as limited in power, perhaps growing with our help. I have noted that what we really lost was our faith in humanity and, since that had effectively taken the place of our faith in God, we thought that our loss of faith in the human race meant the death of God. Still others have suggested that the Holocaust was a unique event, hence inexplicable. If that is so, to try to explain why it happened or what it meant is to deny the horror and thus is itself a sin. There is much to be learned from this ongoing discussion, but it is clear that there is no consensus among Reform Jews or the broader community about what is to be said about the Holocaust. What can and should be said philosophically must therefore be said elsewhere.

Yet one may well argue that this nonintellectual "Nevertheless" is a Jewish answer, for it asserts a faith that drives one to a Jewish life. The Book of Job ends somewhat in this way— though, to be sure, Job has experienced God speaking to him and as a result gives up his questions and confesses his faith. Those of us who have had Job's questions have rarely had his experience. Yet Job's model is not without its traditional Jewish implications. Job never has his questions answered. At the end of his suffering he does not know any more than when he began to question. Despite his lack of understanding, he trusts. Jewish law does not require a Jew in the face of evil to deny the evil or to consider various philosophical explanations as to why evil occurs (though rabbis, philosophers, and mystics have offered them). Instead, it mandates a blessing. The response to evil is an act, something done, not merely thought. One is commanded, amid the trial, to acknowledge God's rule and thereby to deny that this evil event has broken God's order for the universe. Jews may not understand how God permits such things. They are entitled to question and challenge God, as Job did. They are encouraged by the helpful records of their heritage to search for intellectual explanations which may help them relate this trauma to what else they know and believe. But while such philosophy is honored, an act of affirmation is required.

I do not mean by this reference to Jewish law to say that this practice has been easy for traditional Jews or that we moderns can simply follow the old pattern, particularly in the face of so monstrous an evil as the Holocaust. I only want to show that while a philosopher might not consider this Jewish "Nevertheless" an answer, it is a good Jewish way of responding to the problem of evil. In this respect the older Jewish rationalists are a worthy model. They, too, never explained how a good God could have evil in creation. They regularly argued that we must see evil as a challenge to our ethical capacities and answer it by doing the good, by creating righteousness. They thought this was a perfectly rational response to the question of evil, and in some ways it is. But it involves saying that a thinking person can ignore the question of why evil is there, in the world, and not just in the result of a person's faulty will. I am not sure that it is "rational" to have such devotion to duty regardless of one's understanding, but I can easily see its Jewish grounding.

A SENSE OF BELIEF

If we can manage to say "Nevertheless" today, it is, I believe, precisely for historical and cultural reasons. For some time now, ever since Jews in large numbers became university-trained and culturally sophisticated, we have thought of ourselves as essentially agnostic. We preferred mostly not to discuss our lack of belief and often not to act upon it, particularly when we became parents. We set the question of God's reality to one side for the sake of our children and the Jewish community. We liked to think of ourselves as being open to any new evidence for the possibility that God is real, but none ever convinced us. It probably couldn't have. We were always armed with many arguments as to why the evidence couldn't bring us to God. We thought of ourselves religiously as believing, ultimately, nothing. This didn't bother us as long as we could put our trust in culture and see our hopes working out in history. They were our substitute faith. Only now we see (as many Christians do) that history can easily end in ugliness and that culture no longer provides the appropriate values by which people are moved to transform history.

The death-of-God movement of the late 1960s did the entire religious community an unexpected good turn. It announced that God was dead in this culture—but then it could not tell us where a compelling sense of humanity's dignity and destiny was to come from. We were suddenly faced with the possibility that the universe is, at best, neutral and that our goals and standards for human behavior were merely our own idea and nothing more. If that is so, we will not for long do very much about them. We cannot even stay on a diet—because we know we made its rules. But to think of transforming the powerful forces operating in society on the basis of a mere personal inclination is quixotic. Yet, it turns out, we care about people and what happens to humanity. We want our children and our families and our communities and, if at all possible, our country and the world to be humane. We believe in the importance of high human attainment, and we know that this concern is not just our own idea, a childish hope, a cultural remnant, a class interest. Our sense of values, for all that it is shaped by our particular situation, reflects something real and lasting in the universe itself.

It turns out that we do not believe nothing. We are not nihilists. Rather, having come face to face with people who really believe nothing, we have discovered, often to our own amazement, that we believe something. And that is the ground of our "Nevertheless." We do not understand very much indeed about what we mean when we say we have a sense that a transcendent claim is laid upon us—or to put it in simple, traditional language, that there is a God who commands us—but, after all the terrifying experiences of recent decades, that is what we know we believe and probably have believed all along.

I do not deny that there are many other ways for people to find their way to some sense of personal belief and many people whose agnosticism remains in force. But it seems clear to me that the pattern I have described above is characteristic of the recovery of faith by very many people in the Jewish community today.

WHAT BELIEF MUST MEAN

A few additional comments must be made with regard to the content of this affirmation. To have some sense of God means to build your life on it. God is either that important or what one believes in is not God. A religion must be taken that seriously, which is another way of expressing the *Sh'ma*'s "with all your heart, with all your soul, and with all your might." Here the two aspects of modern Jewish living are made explicitly "personal and communal," for to believe as a Jew, while a very personal matter, must likewise include being one of the people of Israel. The foundation is thus laid here for what follows in the *Centenary Perspective* about the Jewish people and one's responsibilities within and to it.

The *Perspective* does not use the term *God's existence* but rather speaks of *God's reality*. The two terms overlap, and the former is avoided in part because it has become something of a cliché and is therefore often treated as if it had no real meaning. There are also some interesting problems raised in modern thought (and incidentally, in his own way, by Maimonides) about what we mean when we speak of God's "existence." The existence we know is of things—but we surely do not mean to imply that God is another thing, just a bigger and better one. So some thinkers have urged us to talk about God as the basis or ground of all existence. That is an elegant point, but the drafters of the *Perspective* had something much simpler in mind: we wanted to say that God was not an illusion, not merely something we imagined, not just a wish of ours. Our God is real, so real that we base our lives on God's reality. By this affirmation we did not mean to close out the possibility that in the future we might draw closer to God in experience or idea. In one sense we remain agnostic: we know we do not know all we can or would like to know about God, and so we remain open to new insights. Even in faith, change remains part of the Jewish experience of God.

CHAPTER FIVE

Of Life after Death

The *Centenary Perspective*'s paragraph on God concludes with a sentence on our belief in life after death. The committee decided to include it here only after some deliberation. Since our hope for an afterlife derives largely from our trust in God, the juxtaposition of the two topics seemed desirable.

TWO INTELLECTUAL PROBLEMS

Most theological matters are not easy to talk about, but the theme of life after death presents two very special problems to modern thinkers. While they may not believe that science knows all about reality, they cannot easily ignore the scientific view of life and thus of death. At present life seems to science essentially a matter of proper chemical combinations. When the right chemicals come together under the right conditions, living matter results. The forms and sizes and structures and capacities of life can grow to extraordinary ranges of complexity, yet they remain, at their base, chemical arrangements. By extension, death is simply the breakdown of a chemical structure which is living. The elements continue on in other configurations, and there is no loss in the total energy in the universe. What is gone is a certain order to which we give the evocative name *life*. As there were only chemicals to begin with, so there are only chemicals afterward. Thus there is no special thing present to survive the death of that most wondrous complex example of life we call a human being. This scientific way of looking at life is dramatically confirmed with every new discovery in molecular biology, and it has made of most religious liberals skeptics if not confirmed disbelievers in life after death.

There is, however, another difficulty related to this topic. In the case of all other religious realities we can claim some personal experience, be it of a rational or of a more feeling variety. There is nothing analogous about our hope for life after death. Of course, this is what makes research into psychic phenomena so intriguing, particularly when there is contact with someone who has died or with a person's previous existence. Were we able to validate such data, we could then not only affirm the reasonableness of religious belief in an afterlife but we could insist that scientists acknowledge this data and rethink their theory of human life so as to account for it. Thus far the results of research in this realm have been inconclusive. They surely do not seem to warrant basing one's religious faith on them. While leaving the question of possible personal experience open, then, one finds oneself without a basis upon which to base one's belief.

THE NEED FOR A STATEMENT

These two intellectual problems are reinforced by the Jewish tradition's reluctance to say much about life after death and by the modern religious thinker's concern to keep the focus of religion on this world and our responsibilities in it. The result has been that most Jews in our time avoid speaking about personal survival after death. Mostly there is talk about living on in the memory of those who knew one or, for those of a rationalist bent, one can speak of people living on in the ethical deeds they did. It came as no surprise, then, that the question was raised in our committee (and by several rabbis who responded to the first draft circulated) as to whether this topic required a statement at all. For many people it is a matter of little or no importance. Since many matters could not be commented on, the absence of a statement on life after death would not prove disturbing. The committee, though conscious of the intellectual problems it faced and how little it could honestly say in their face, decided it could not pass this matter by. Though many Reform Jews are agnostic or disbelieving in this area, the committee felt that such positive faith as could be given utterance deserved a place in the statement.

DESCRIPTIONS OF LIFE

Those who affirm life after death emphatically reject the notion that human life can ever adequately be described in chemical terms alone. No one denied that analyzing life in terms of its chemistry has had many useful results or that great benefits would yet result from extending chemical research into life. The delicate question is not whether talking about human life in chemical terms is useful, but only whether one can go on from what we know to say, "It is only chemical." Yet we have no alternate way of talking about human life that tells us very much about its origins, maintenance, or end.

In this respect the Bible and the thinkers of the Middle Ages (who reinforced the Bible's views with certain philosophical notions) were very much better off than we are. They believed that a human life resulted from the combination of two parts, a body and a soul. For them the soul was a thing, what in the Middle Ages was called a substance, which was eternal. When one died, God took the soul back to a special realm, at some later date to be inserted into the restored body at the resurrection for the final judgment and the disposition of the person.

Whether one wishes to replace the concept of resurrection with that of the immortality of the soul or not, our present difficulty is that the notion of such a substance as a soul is no longer intellectually tenable for most modern thinkers. If one wants to talk about survival after death, it would be helpful to be able to say just what survives, what it is beside chemicals (or somehow extant through the chemicals) which makes up the unique thing we call human life. Earlier in this century it was still possible to use the term *spirit*, for it had some status in the German philosophical world on which America drew so heavily. From this came the heavy Reform Jewish emphasis on immortality. But by now *spirit* has gone the way of *soul*. We still use both words—but only poetically, to point to what we think we believe but have very little idea of. So with regard to the "mechanics" of life after death we have almost nothing to say and, at the moment, we have no good prospects for explaining life so as to clarify why we believe it does not end for us once we die. No wonder so many Jews have given up this belief.

LIFE AS MYSTERY

Yet a positive sense of an afterlife can be derived, if not from ourselves then from our relationship with God and our sense of God's reality. We are indeed creatures, but creatures of a most exalted capacity. We are conscious not merely of our own reality but of that of God, the supreme reality of all existence. There is something about our life which can respond to, and in that sense participate in, God's reality. We know ourselves to be called upon by God in ways that, so far as we can tell, extend to no other creatures. We are God's coworkers in nature. So, in our limited way, we share in God's purposes and power. All creatures share in God's reality; we do so in special measure. Through the phenomena of our consciousness, our intellect, our will, our personhood we come to know ourselves as especially close to God's own reality. There is something God-like about human beings, and God does not die. We have no name for this special character of human life. We do not know its relationship to our chemical nature. Indeed, science and Judaism seem to be talking in two radically different ways about what it is to be a person, and this may necessarily prevent any synthesis of them. Yet even as we have good reason for not denying the chemical understanding of much of our existence, so we have good reason for not denying the reality and greater significance of our special relationship to God.

In this Jewish view, life is seen as a mystery. When we understand it with the greatest precision, chemically, it is utterly different from our immediate personal experience of it. The elements have no will or consciousness, yet from them is supposed to derive our inner life. They are utterly amoral and apparently unesthetic. We consider people without a moral sense and devoid of appreciation for beauty somehow unhuman. Perhaps there are scientific ways of explaining how multiplying and ordering packets of programmed energy eventually yield persons. The topic of how matter yields spirit is still hotly debated. To the religious mind the idea that chemicals, in no matter how complex a configuration, should ever have been spoken of as possessing a soul is indicative of a mystery built into creation. Taken at its fullest, we do not understand life. We accept its mysteriously given limits and opportunities and try to work within them.

DEATH AS MYSTERY

Death is a greater mystery. We do not know life without a physical base. We have no experience of what existence the other side of death could be like. Against that ignorance we balance our recognition that life itself is mysterious, that death is part of life and the creation God ordained. Death, like life, comes from the God whom we know daily showers goodness on us. We trust God's goodness even in death. We cannot believe that having shared so intimately in God's reality in life we do not continue to share it beyond the grave. Our creaturely existence, having risen to the level of participating in the ultimate reality in the universe, God's, now may aspire to extend and fulfill that greatness it came partially to know in life. Having reached such heights precisely in our personhood, our individuality, we trust that our survival likewise will be personal and individual.

Searching for a way of pointing to the intimate relationship between God and people, the committee gave up its normal use of modern terms and utilized a biblical metaphor: human beings are said to be "created in God's image." The phrase is familiar enough to convey our sense of the closeness between God and people. Yet its biblical provenance is sufficiently well known that this sudden, unusual metaphorical reference should signal a special form of religious affirmation. What *image* means cannot be defined, but after centuries of significant usage the term is not empty of content. We cannot say very clearly what we believe, yet we do not propose to abandon our faith that the God who gave us life will yet give us life after death.

This is a most modest affirmation—one sentence with its several evocative but limited terms. For all that, it is an important belief for those of us who share it to acknowledge and articulate. Perhaps that is the way of modern Jewish faith. We find ourselves unable to say very much. But we are able to say something. So what we do say is very important.

PART III

The People Israel

The Jewish people and Judaism defy precise definition because both are in the process of becoming. Jews, by birth or conversion, constitute an uncommon union of faith and peoplehood. Born as Hebrews in the ancient Near East, we are bound together like all ethnic groups by language, land, history, culture, and institutions. But the people of Israel is unique because of its involvement with God and its resulting perception of the human condition. Throughout our long history our people has been inseparable from its religion with its messianic hope that humanity will be redeemed.

From the Centenary Perspective

CHAPTER SIX

Why Is There
No Statement on Human Nature?

BEGINNING WITH THE PARTICULAR

The second paragraph of the *Centenary Perspective*'s "principles" again shows how this document stresses the social side of being Jewish. This impression arises not simply because this is a paragraph on the Jewish people or because so ethnic a matter immediately follows the discussion of God. Almost everyone would expect a Reform Jewish statement today to have a positive feeling for the Jewish folk, and it seems natural to us to talk about the Jewish people after talking about God. Yet this means that nothing much has been said—certainly it is not one of the principles—about human nature generally, about people as a whole and their relationship to God. The document speaks only about the Jews, this one group and its involvement with God.

The liberals of another day would have followed a different pattern. They regularly started from universal human experience and then worked their way up to a belief in God. Since all people were capable of knowing God and none had special ability or unique experiences, whatever was to be said about the Jews had to derive from the general possibilities of being human. Humanity logically came before the Jewish people—as it did in many liberal lives—and that is the order which is followed in the first great modern book on Jewish theology, Kaufmann Kohler's book of that title. (Since Kohler was president of the Hebrew Union College, his formulation, about the time of World War I, was highly influential among Reform Jews, though other liberal thinkers held similar ideas.) Anyone familiar with the previous point of view might well wonder why the *Centenary Perspective* speaks of the Jewish people without first clarifying the universal human situation.

PERSONAL COMMITMENT

The response is substantially the same as that given to the parallel question: What happened to individualism in the paragraph on God? There, the focus was on God's place in the people of Israel's will to survive rather than God's relationship with all humanity. Here, rather than speaking of what individuals in general—humanity—can know about God and do in God's service, the concern is again the Jewish people. With space limited, the message of this hour is highlighted, much else being taken for granted. What is critical to Reform as to all Jewish experience in our time is the involve-

ment of the individual Jew with the Jewish
people. This major theme of the *Perspective* is
reiterated here to special effect. With reference
to universal humanity left in the background
while Jewish ethnicity is given center stage, a
rebuke is administered to those who insist they
can be Jewish in utter privacy. Instead, the
rabbis are here saying that a proper Jewish life
is not limited to what one does in one's heart,
though one should put one's heart into it. As
against Whitehead's maxim on being religious,
Jewish existence is not what one does with
one's solitariness, even though it obviously
starts with the individual. To be a Jew is to be
part of a people, and without involvement in
Jewish peoplehood one can not be much of a
Jew.

Fortunately, this folk encourages all sorts of
individuality, so that having a mind of one's
own and doing things in one's own style has
long largely been honored among Jews, and
certainly so in modern times. But trying to be a
Jew without benefit of our folk history or
tradition or present community but only as
some sort of person-in-general is rather a contradiction in terms. Of course one can be a
"kosher Jew" on a desert island or in some
other situation where isolation is enforced.
Thus without a minyan, one can still pray—but,
symbolically enough, one prays what the minyan would be praying, with some exceptions,
and, preferably, about the time a normal

minyan would be praying it. You may be
forced to be all alone—yet you live your life in
relation to the community of Israel. Going further, you may certainly say your own, private
prayers to God whenever you want to (and in a
special part of the regular service), but that is
no substitute for the common Jewish duty; an
individual Jew must join with the community
in the shared, corporate action of his people.

THE EXAGGERATED INDIVIDUAL

At this centenary hour the old Reform Jewish
emphasis on the individual seems so secure—it
is so fundamental a premise it comes up again
and again in the *Centenary Perspective*—that it
did not seem to require fresh, explicit treatment. The opposite rather seems to be the case.
Individualism has come to dominate our self-
consciousness to the point that our social
nature and responsibility are often ignored. In
America today the widespread criterion of
value is "What's in it for me?" The old counterbalancing sense of the common good has substantially been given up in the name of an
alleged realism. What begins sensibly enough as
an education that tries to meet student needs
expands by inescapable, seductive advertising
into the subconscious expectation that the
world centers around us and exists for our
gratification. Operating on the basis of such a
fantasy one can hardly understand why
marriage, the synagogue, or the community

makes such great demands; illusion blinds us to the simple truth that our vaunted singleness would not amount to much if there weren't a whole culture and society to give it a basis and context. Totalitarianism has sacrificed the individual to the nation, but one often has the impression in the democracies these days that the world and society exist mainly to nurse us.

The Jewish equivalent of this exaggerated individualism is the radical separation of one's self as person from oneself as Jew. Then one can believe that what one really cares about and hopes to achieve has little to do with one's having been born into the Jewish people. So one takes up the consumer's stand toward Jewish life, asking always, "What's in it for me—now?" Obviously, the *Centenary Perspective* does not mean to assert a totalitarian Jewish standard, that the individual Jew exists for the sake of the Jewish people whose corporate dictates should supersede all personal concerns. It rather hopes to correct the mistaken notion that most of us would be what we are as individuals without our Jewish background—consider how critical ethnicity is to our odd statistics of social achievement—and that the Jewish tradition exists only to serve our needs and not, legitimately, also to make certain claims upon us.

As long as one keeps a gulf between one's essential self and one's merely accidental Jewishness, one will never have a healthy sense of what it is to be a Jew. Thus what needs attention in the present stage of American Reform Judaism is not so much the loss of our general individuality to the social mass, as bad a problem as that is, but the erosion of our self-identification with the Jewish people as the result of an overblown individualism.

CONFLICTS OF CONSCIENCE

Stressing so the ethnic side of our individuality, the *Centenary Perspective* might very well have gone on to explore the problems which arise for a sensitive Jew when personal fulfillment conflicts with group responsibility. On the everyday level such issues come up whenever hobbies, excursions, or fatigue conflict with services, study, or community meetings. Sometimes a Jewish conscience is torn between the sense that two children are all that this family rightfully should bring into the world and another that this number is at least one less than replenishing the Jewish people makes mandatory.

No conflict of duty to self and to community in our time is as classic as that raised by the possibility of intermarriage. If one is essentially responsible to one's self, and if one's fundamental duty is self-fulfillment, then, in this trying time, one should marry whomever one might reasonably hope to live out one's life in happiness with. Naturally, both partners being Jewish might make that somewhat easier, and it would surely be more rich ethnically. But if the self is primary, and if being Jewish is nice but marginal, then the future spouse's non-Jewish background will not matter much to us. However, if our individuality and Jewishness are closely interrelated, then not to marry a Jew would be a betrayal of self. Of course, the *Perspective* does not discuss the intermarriage issue. I have only brought up this thorny topic to illustrate how the emphasis on individualism can lead to certain tensions in Jewish duty. Since the majority of Reform rabbis are on record as opposing the performance of intermarriage, I imagine they will interpret the weight given here to the group rather than the individual as an endorsement of their position.

Yet if, as the *Perspective*'s paragraph on diversity noted, people should interpret the statements here in their own thoughtful and conscientious Reform Jewish way, another view will certainly be forthcoming. This document is not against the individualism long emphasized by Reform Judaism. It rather takes it for granted in most of what it says. With regard to intermarriage, the ethnic concern of the document means only that people who approach things in terms of themselves should also consider at the time of marriage their relationship to the Jewish people and their obligations to it. Many rabbis who perform intermarriages certainly hope that such considerations will be part of a couple's thinking in approaching marriage. Such rabbis conduct an intermarriage in the hope of gaining a family and their children for the Jewish people. They thus see themselves as no less loyal to the Jewish people and no less concerned with its importance in the lives of individuals than are their nonintermarrying colleagues. The paragraph on "The People Israel" also bespeaks their view, though they draw different consequences from it than do the majority of their colleagues, including me.

This is a good example of the diversity engendered by the double affirmations of Reform Judaism—here self and people. Though this is an unusually emotional and disturbing matter to those in the antagonistic parties, it also illustrates with unusual clarity how unity often lies behind Reform Jewish dissension. All the disputants affirm the significance of the Jewish people in the life of the individual Jew and feel that it deserves more emphasis in our time than it received in the recent past. Yet everyone also agrees that the believing, knowledgeable self-determining individual is the basis of Reform Judaism.

CHAPTER SEVEN

Why Is Defining the Jews so Difficult?

COMPLEX HISTORICAL DATA

Trying to explain who the Jews are or what Judaism is becomes troublesome for two reasons: the variegated data and the descriptive terms available. Consider the Jews of Bible times. They began as a family which eventually grew into tribes and clans. They wandered in the wilderness like bedouin, then settled as a loosely federated group of tribes living in a land they occupied. Then they were, in turn, a nation under a king, a few tribes in exile, a small group of returnees living as a special religious group as part of a great empire—and they show other social patterns as well. Racial, religious, and national factors all play a role in these portraits of the Jews, though in an extraordinarily varied mix. The result is that one historically continuous group took on many forms, at times quite different one from the other.

One must then add to the biblical data the utterly unexpected historical phenomenon that this people was then detached from its ancestral land for nearly two thousand years and scattered all over near Asia, Europe, North

Africa, and the Americas. In these millennia
there was no single continuing center of physical existence, but only shifting points of religious preeminence. Already the problem of
simple description is well out of hand. But then
the Jews reconstituted themselves as a nation
in the Land of Israel, though Jews around the
world have no political share in it!

Thus to say that the people of Israel has
been a dynamic phenomenon, changing and
adapting its social nature over the centuries,
is an understatement. But definitions are
static. A word which was adequate to the Jews
in one time is rarely accurate to describe them
a while later. Today, with Jews thinking of
themselves in many varied ways, definition is
all the more hazardous.

COMPLEX RELIGIOUS DATA

Matters are equally complex when one tries to
find a simple word with which to describe the
relationship of this people to God. In their
classic period their God involves them with a
land, in the creation of a certain kind of
society, and is deeply concerned with their
politics as well as with a cult in a great central
sanctuary. Then all of this disappears and is
replaced by a religion of lawyers—and preachers called rabbis, some of whom are wonder-
workers and others of whom are mystics,
though mysticism is later challenged by a
philosophical development that considers the

nonrational dangerous. In modern times this construction substantially gives way when the majority of Jews no longer observes rabbinic law or respects rabbinic authority. Equally difficult, some modern conceptions of a proper Jewish relationship to God go far beyond the admittedly wide range of rabbinically permitted interpretations, while a very large number of Jews claim not to be believers at all. If, then, this is a "religion," it is a most odd one.

JUDAISM AS "RELIGION"

The variety of Jewish social and religious experience is staggering. Our culture simply has no word to describe so multifaceted a phenomenon, almost certainly because our language has been shaped so strongly by Christianity. Its particular experience of God is adopted as the model for people's relationship to God. The affect of this Christianizing of our general language is widespread. A good deal of what seems the essential similarity of world religions often derives from our translating the texts of other faiths, including primitive ones, using English terms with a Christian conception of God and piety behind them. So other sacred books naturally come out sounding reminiscent of the Bible.

The most immediately appealing English word we could use to describe the Jews, particularly in terms of their concern with the life

of the spirit, is *religion.* In many ways that
gives a good sense of the historical Jewish
experience, but only if one does not press the
notion very hard. There is the odd biblical
involvement with land, society, and government; there are the anomalies of contemporary
Jewish disbelief and the secular but Jewish
State of Israel. The problem with using the
word *religion* for the Jews is that it customarily
implies a "church." Christians have a special
sense of religion, and it derives logically from
the unique events which gave rise to their faith.
The Christ comes into the world to begin transforming the normal perception of affairs and to
save people. Hence Christians are those drawn
forth from humanity by their faith and the
grace of God. Obviously, that is too limited a
statement of a great and complex doctrine.
Still, it will serve to indicate how, for a Christian, religion is a matter of having the right
faith and, variously understood, being part of
the right group, the Church. In such a view,
religion implies accepting the creed or the
dogmas which clarify what constitutes a saving
faith and participating in the group created on
the basis of finding faith, the Church.

Not every *religion* is easily understood as a
church. The Buddhists may more easily be
described as sharing a rather rationally arrived-
at philosophy, and they are socially organized
around their monastic brotherhood. For
Muslims, religion is not so much located in a

separate activity—which, to be sure, is supposed to influence all of life—but is really coextensive with cultural and national life. I think it fair to say that in the history of religion the Christian way of thinking about believers and their relationship to God is somewhat unusual. In any case, the Jews are not a church. They are not organized around a saving faith, and efforts to identify a Jewish creed of Jewish dogmas have normally met with intense debate and little acceptance. Moreover, the Jewish group is far more inclusive of activities and interests than what we normally expect of a church. Thus, the word *religion*, which is our normal English term for a relationship to God, is somewhat misleading, even in that limited focus, when applied to the Jews. When one adds to this spiritual inadequacy a full acceptance of what we have come to call the ethnic realities of Jewish life, *religion* covers perhaps a major dimension of Jewish existence, and that with some possible distortion, but surely not the whole thing.

THE ETHNIC-RELIGIOUS SEPARATION

This split of the religious from the ethnic side of being Jewish demands special comment. Even in the few biblical examples given above it was clear that faith and nation were utterly intertwined. As a result of the Emancipation, the usual source of our modern Jewish problems, they were radically separated. Had the

Jews come out of the ghetto into a world where religion was, as it had been, a major ingredient of culture, the issue might not have arisen. In the medieval period, the nature of the Jews as a group was not a serious question. Maimonides in his thirteen principles of Jewish belief does not mention the Jewish people. (Check the *Yigdal* hymn or its translation in the prayerbook the next time you are at services for a song version of Maimonides' "creed.") Maimonides and other Jewish thinkers did not have to talk directly about the Jewish people, because in their day the major divisions among humankind were seen as essentially religious or, to be more precise, as the result of different revelations. The Torah had its followers, as did the Koran and the New Testament. Philosophers were therefore mainly concerned with explaining how revelation could occur and arguing why one's group had the true one. Only when religion is not taken seriously and revelation becomes problematic do thinkers shift their focus from what God did in order to separate humanity into groups to what sorts of divisions have naturally arisen among human beings. Secularism set the context for the emancipation of the Jews and thus the possibility of thinking of them as a natural social group on the one hand and as a church-like religious group on the other.

The people who created the idea of a secular state, one where religion is separate from citizenship, did not know whether Jews could take part in such an arrangement. Before the French Revolution most people knew that the Jews lived separate from the general populace. Jews had been, so to speak, a nation within the nation, conducting their own law courts and collecting their own taxes for the government. Gentile society did not realize how much this was due to its segregation and persecution of the Jews over centuries. Instead, the non-Jews projected an image of extreme clannishness, even of the hatred of humanity, onto the Jews. When they had to face the issue of equal rights for Jews, they wanted to know, with varying levels of anti-Semitic hostility, on what basis Jews were now to take part in the state. There were no longer to be separate groups within the free, western European nations, but only one people—say, the French or the British, and somewhat later the German. One could legitimately maintain one's separateness only on a religious basis—that is, if one was a Protestant (in varying denomination) or a Catholic, the major religious divisions. If the Jews wished to fully partake of the new national life—a possibility of incredible promise to the ghetto dwellers—they could be separate as a religion but not as another nation. When Napoleon asked leaders of French Jewry for an official Jewish community response to the offer of citizenship, he specifically asked them whether their religion permitted or placed barriers in the way of their full participation in the new French nation. In effect, he wanted to know if they were a religion sufficiently like Protestantism and Catholicism, to be granted the private privilege of separate existence. They answered as have the Jews of almost every free country ever since that time. They identified themselves as such a religion. In due course a word was coined for this; in English, it is *Judaism.* We could avoid a number of misconceptions if we remembered how recent that term is and under what circumstances it came into being. I am not sure how much of an "ism" the Jews have had—but saying we were *Judaism,* a religion, made the social side of being Jewish even more difficult to describe.

EQUALITY AT THE EXPENSE OF ETHNICITY

The very way the question is now put produces both the benefits of the new situation and its problems. Dividing the state and citizenship from religious belief—specifically, making it non-Christian—means that Jews can be part of it and yet carry on as a separate religion. But splitting nationality and religion also makes it impossible for Jews to say that in their religion the believers are not a church but an ethnic group, what Europeans might call a nationality. To gain entry into the Western world the Jews had to suppress a part of their Jewish identity. This was so sensitive a matter while the Jews

were struggling for their rights that the Reform
Jews turned their relationship to the Land of
Israel and their concern for the coming of the
King-Messiah into empty symbols rather than
historical expectations. Subsequent history has
convinced most Jews that our attitude toward
our Land and to self-government should not be
so abstractly idealized, but is something Jews
can and should do something about here and
now.

What have remained troublesome are the
limits this modern sense of being a Jew had
imposed on our community life. We have synagogues and voluntary organizations as Christians do. We go beyond that to organize
community councils for defense, fundraising,
some coordination of activity, and a bit of
joint planning. But the concept of our being
another religious community and the limited
role for ethnic groups in a democracy do not
allow for very much more than that. If the
Jews, however, for all their religious tradition,
are also a people with a rich folk tradition and
need to live out their religiosity in diverse corporate ways, then they lost a good deal while
making the gains of coming into the democratic state.

THE RESTORATION OF ETHNICITY

The Jews of the nineteenth and early twentieth
centuries who were struggling to win equality
could not say, as we do so easily today, "We

are another religion, but we happen to be organized as an ethnic group and not as a church." In their day such words hadn't yet come into general use, because the concept of maintaining separate ethnic groups was utterly unacceptable. Jewish thinkers groped for modern words that could usefully describe the Jewish group. They were quite interested when, in the latter part of the nineteenth century, the concept of race came into intellectual fashion. Here was a scientific term which explained differences between peoples in a way which didn't interfere with their participating in their states—at least until the Germans began to apply race to nationality. By the early part of the twentieth century it had been adopted by Jewish thinkers as diverse as Kaufmann Kohler in the United States and Franz Rosenzweig and Martin Buber in Germany. Today we shudder at their use of such terms as *Jewish blood*—which they believed transmitted the genetic information. But we are speaking out of the horrors we saw done in the name of race, while they were speaking out of the relatively harmless, limited, social vocabulary of their time.

Our present vocabulary is the result of something of a revolution in the American consciousness. As long as Americans thought in terms of democracy as a "melting pot," ethnic diversity seemed culturally backward. Then to have described the Jews as *ethnic* would have meant that they were still attached to their immigrant roots. But as Americans began to value group existence—as it became clear that Blacks and Indians, Poles and Italians, Greeks and other nationalities had a right to preserve and foster their specific heritage, thereby enriching our democracy—one could use the word *ethnic* to describe the Jewish group and expect that it would be positively received.

AN IDEA OF WHO WE ARE

This still doesn't settle our problem of defining the Jews. Even if we are a most peculiar group. Other such groups are primarily racial or national, but we still claim to be a religion. In the modern, democratic sense we are a religious group, but our social base is ethnic. Thus we seem to have two parts to us, which have become separated and which we somehow cannot put back together. The Western world has no good term for such a group, mostly because there aren't very many of them. (Below I shall discuss an Asian group with similar characteristics, the Sikhs.) The problem set for us by the Emancipation remains: our nationality derives from our citizenship and our separateness essentially from our religion, though this happens to have an ethnic, not a church, base. This is a clumsy way to try to understand oneself, and it is clumsier still to use in trying to explain it to someone who has not lived it. No wonder we have such difficulty making clear to Christians why we are so involved with what they see as only a political entity, the State of Israel. Nonetheless, though we cannot be precise or elegant, we now have some words which give a fairly adequate idea of who the Jews are—at least for the time being.

CHAPTER EIGHT

The Double Affirmation: Faith and Peoplehood

BEING BORN A JEW

Perhaps nothing so well demonstrates what seems to the Christian mentality the strange double nature of the Jews as the two ways one becomes a Jew, birth or conversion. Birth is not easily thought of as a way to enter a church where accepting a saving faith is critical. Some Protestants insist that one cannot properly join the church until one is mature enough personally to accept the Christ. (Catholics deal with this by the sacrament of confirmation.) Other Christians, basing themselves on the New Testament accounts, accept infants into the church by baptism. This can lead to the troublesome status of the child born to Christian parents who dies before being baptized. In Christianity the biological act of being born cannot substitute for baptism or accepting the faith. But a Jew is born Jewish, traditionally, if born to a Jewish mother. The biological nature of this is borne out by the analogous case of the Jewish male infant who is not circumcised for legitimate reasons (e.g., health) and who then dies. There is no question of the status of

73

that child. He died fully a Jew and has as much hope for the afterlife as any other Jew. Circumcision is a major law, but it is not a condition of being a Jew (and certainly not a sacrament, an act in which God fully participates, since Judaism has no such rites). Neither the traditional naming ceremony for girls in the synagogue nor the circumcision of males makes children Jewish. Birth does.

Entry into a group by birth is natural for an ethnic group. Americans easily understand that the child of Italian parents, say third-generation Chicagoans, is "an Italian." Obviously that child is not a citizen of Italy but of the United States. Yet if the family is at all concerned with its origin and the perpetuation of the customs connected with it, the child will have the sort of ethnic background implied by the term *Italian.* This is so common that it seems somewhat old-fashioned, because unnecessarily defensive, to hyphenate the child as an Italian-American. So in terms of normal entry into the group the Jews are obviously ethnic. But then, too, people become Jews by conversion.

CONVERTING TO JUDAISM

By contrast to the birth route the conversion path of entry into the Jews is easily understood by Christians. Leaving aside now the difference between the special Christian sense of "seeing the light" and speaking merely of the notion of gaining a faith one did not have before, conversion is the classic Christian way of entering a religion. So converts to Judaism seem to follow a well-known path and Judaism appears to be a religion. One can make something of a case that conversion to Judaism is more like changing ethnic groups than like accepting faith in a Christian way. Traditionally what one does for would-be proselytes is to remind them of all the problems the Jewish people undergoes and then, if they persist, to instruct them in the Jewish way of life. Once they learn what Jews do and agree to do this wholeheartedly, they are accepted in our midst, a process not dissimilar to becoming a citizen of another country. But while one may want to distinguish the Jewish sense of religion from the Christian and thus emphasize its ethnic aspects, one cannot ignore the relationship to God which lies at the heart of sincere Jewish observance. If the traditional pattern of conversion did not include direct theological instruction, that was because it could be assumed that Jewish practice would carry the message of Jewish belief to the convert as it did to Jews. An insincere convert, a mechanical, unbelieving *mitzvah*-doer, could not properly be called a convert to Judaism. Ruth, the Moabitess, whom the rabbis considered the classic model of a genuine convert, put the dimensions of being a Jew beautifully when she is described as saying to her mother-in-law, Naomi, "Thy people shall be my people, and thy God, my God."

SPIRITUAL AND BIOLOGICAL

If, then, the spiritual component is critical to being a Jew, it is reasonably clear how an act of conversion can bring one to it; but then what has biology to do with it? Being born to Jewish parents may bring you into an ethnic group, but can it automatically bring you into some sort of relationship with God? The matter can be taken to what seems, to the outsider, an almost absurd level. A woman born to gentile parents is not Jewish. She then, by learning and will, converts to Judaism. But then, purely biologically, her child is born Jewish. The child gets by birth what the parent received only by will—yet it seems inconceivable that the mother's decision to be a Jew had changed her biology and made it "Jewish"! Incidentally, something of a similar oddity operates in the opposite direction. Though you may become a Jew by conversion, you cannot remove yourself from the Jewish people by converting to another faith. You may lose certain rights and privileges within the Jewish community as a result of your apostasy, but when you are ready to come back we will not ask you to undergo conversion. You may have to undertake some acts which indicate the genuineness of your return, and some authorities have been known to impose penalties for such sinfulness. Still, the rule usually applied here is "A Jew who sins is still a Jew." (The case is slightly different with a gentile convert who later leaves

Judaism. They are generally not still considered Jews but rather people whose conversion was probably not truly sincere to begin with. Decisions on such cases will vary, but often the ethnic tie does not hold them when the religious tie lapses.) It is also remarkable how often when Jews convert to another faith their Jewish identity clings to them. Perhaps this is due to the anti-Semitism of those who refuse to forget the Jew's origins. Yet it is also testimony to the special ethnic way one is a Jew and should not be utterly discounted.

A UNION OF PEOPLEHOOD AND FAITH

With all this in mind the *Centenary Perspective* calls the Jews an "uncommon union of faith and peoplehood." *Unique* would have been too strong a term. Among those whom anthropologists once used to call primitive peoples, the union of religion and ethnicity is the norm, not the exception. What makes the Jews radically different from such groups is the universal nature of the Jewish God and the almost worldwide experience of the Jewish people. Most other groups whose religion was coextensive with their culture had a rather limited sense of God and lived in one small area. Already in biblical times the Jews believed that there was one God in all the world and that God was the God of their people in a very special and intimate way. Even when the Jews left their native land through exile and dispersion, they still retained this faith. Losing the normal attributes of nationality, they did not give up their ethnicity.

At least one other group has had so comprehensive a sense of God, what historians of religion have termed "a high God," and yet insisted that the group who served this God most appropriately was fundamentally national in character. The Sikhs are a people of India who in the sixteenth century were brought to a new religion by the guru Nanak. The ethnic character of their faith is most readily seen in their distinctive dress. Sikh males wear turbans, have beards, and carry some metal on them. While one can join the Sikhs, their own children are born into the Sikh "faith" as into the Sikh nation. The similarities with the Jews are quite real. Defenders of Jewish uniqueness will insist that the Sikh experience is too short to be compared to that of the Jews and that the Sikhs have never undergone the ultimate test of the ethnicity of their religiosity, namely the destruction of their major institutions in their homeland and dispersion from it. The two cases are somewhat different. With all that, the Sikhs show that the sort of union the Jews have between ethnicity and religion is not otherwise unknown in human religion.

To people growing up in a Christian environment it may seem somewhat odd that faith and peoplehood, will and biology, can interact the way they do among the Jews. Nonetheless, that is the Jewish way and it has its parallels among other peoples. There have not been enough cases to make such groups worthy of a distinctive descriptive term. This leaves one with the need to create special coinages for Sikh-Jewish-type groups. We are left with such hybrid usages as *religioethnic* or *ethnic-religious,* and thus the vocabulary of the English language itself turns out to be a special Jewish problem.

CHAPTER NINE

Some Ways in Which We Are Ethnic

HEBREW—THE JEWISH LANGUAGE

Aside from entry by birth, ethnicity operates among Jews in a number of ways, some of which the *Centenary Perspective* specifies. The first is language—most obviously, these days, Hebrew. If one compares the role of Hebrew among the Jews to Latin among Roman Catholics, the ethnic factor quickly emerges. No one has ever suggested, to the best of my knowledge, that the cause of Catholic Christianity would be much better served if all Catholics could be gotten to speak, read, and write in Latin, but that surely has been the goal of Jewish Hebraists. Indeed, I think 'most American Jews would agree that were it possible somehow easily to achieve it, we would have far better Jews in this country if all of us were fully at ease in the Hebrew language.

Of course in Protestant Christianity, a special language plays no role at all. Perhaps the issue would be put more clearly if I distinguished between what Protestants have called an ethnic church and the sort of ethnicity which is critical to Jewish religiosity. An ethnic church is generally identified as one that largely utilizes the language of the immigrants who founded it—German, Swedish, or the like. When the immigrant generation passes, some traces of the old ethnic style may linger on. Generally this is not the use of the old language, since most Americans tend not to use their parents' and grandparents' native tongues. Rather, what remains is the style of the church, its celebrations, special events and foods, perhaps too a special concern with the interpretation of Christianity current in the old homeland. But when the church is fully Americanized, when English is spoken and the children of this church move on to other churches without these old-country ties, one cannot say that the church or its wandering offspring are now less Christian. The ethnicity was not critical to the religiosity but an addendum to it. Among Jews a similar case would be the use of German in the synagogues of the late-nineteenth-century American immigrants. It was a functioning part of their Jewishness, but they could give it up and still remain quite authentically Jewish.

Whether one could give up Hebrew completely and for all time and still remain significantly a Jew is quite doubtful. Better than such theoretical speculations, however, is the experience of Reform Judaism in the United States. There were some rabbis and congregations early in the century who almost completely dispensed with the Hebrew language. Their argument was that one should not pray in words one did not understand, that God would surely accept prayers on the basis of intention rather than in consideration of the tongue in which they were uttered. Yet despite the logic of these statements, the Reform movement has since the turn of the century steadily moved in a more Hebraic direction· Prayer should be heartfelt, but Jewish prayer includes joining one's heart with the hearts of one's people and, through their words, to the hearts of those Jews who by their faithful continuity made possible one's own Jewish life. So for some years now Reform Jews have generally asked that their services include a number of Hebrew prayers whose words they may not directly understand yet which they want to hear. They know that Hebrew binds them tightly to the Jewish people and thus is intimately related to Jewish belief and practice, a good instance of the uncommon link of ethnicity and belief among us.

OTHER JEWISH LANGUAGES

The linguistic factor in Jewish ethnicity is not limited to Hebrew. The Jews have had a proclivity for creating languages down through the ages. Of these mixtures of Hebrew with a vernacular, American Jews are most familiar with Yiddish, though the Sephardim among us will speak or remember Ladino. There are good records and occasional speakers of other Jewish languages—Judeo-Persian, Judeo-Arabic, and such. That is hardly the sort of thing a religion, in the Christian sense, should have been doing, yet the Jews regularly created distinctive literatures and folklores in a number of such special languages over the centuries.

Maurice Samuel had a delightful theory about Yiddish which, if true, lends extra testimony to the Jewish mix of ethnicity and religion. He suggested that Yiddish was invented, so to speak, to keep a measure of Hebrew alive in the everyday lives of Jews. Yiddish has been variously estimated as carrying about 20 percent of its vocabulary in borrowed Hebrew words. A Jew who speaks Yiddish already is in touch with a substantial Hebrew vocabulary. Though the sacred tongue itself had been limited to religious life activities, it was carried over into the secular activities of Jews by being incorporated into a special Jewish language.

ISRAEL—THE JEWISH LAND

The Land of Israel has long occupied a special place in the Jewish religion and its life. The Bible has made Jerusalem more than a city for countless people around the world and Zion more than a hill therein. These ordinary places have been transformed by Jewish and Christian experience into symbols of the transcendent, locales where God and people came into special

contact. How much the more have they meant
to Jews whose folk had its origins on that land,
who considered it part of their unique relationship with God, and who looked to it as the site
where the redemption of their people and all
humanity would center.

Reform Jews of an earlier time had difficulty with this classic Jewish emphasis on the
Land of Israel. Facing the suspicions of the
new nations who cautiously gave them rights or
of neighbors who wondered if Jews were not
congenital aliens, the early Reform Jews elimi-
nated prayers for a return to the Land of Israel
from their prayerbook. But they did not
eliminate—could anyone?—the Land of Israel
from their Judaism. They still cherished the
Bible and thus retained steady contact with its
strangely evocative places. They maintained the
Jewish calendar with its associations with the
agricultural cycle of the old homeland. Thus
Reform Jews made no effort to do away with
Sukkot but took great pride in its relation to
the Puritan and later American festival of
Thanksgiving. Yet in these latitudes, giving God
thanks for the harvest in late September or
early October made sense only if one explained
that we celebrated here now as our people did
in Bible days in the Land of Israel. It took the
horror of the Hitler years and the joys associated with the establishment of the State of
Israel, as well as the new American appreciation of ethnicity, to let the Land of Israel come

to a fuller place in Reform Judaism. The *Centenary Perspective* seems to take for granted that acceptance of the Land of Israel as one more facet of the rounded-out Reform Judaism of our times. Since a common land is a major factor in ethnicity, it is listed here among the things that Jews, in their ethnic aspect, share.

THE JEWISH STYLE

The *Perspective* goes on to list "history, culture, and institutions." It could have added a good deal more, and these must be considered merely a few major indications of Jewish ethnicity. Each in turn could be broken down into many parts. So in a discussion of institutions we could discuss those peculiarly interesting creations, the Jewish family or school or community structure. All ethnic groups have them and give them their own distinctive twist. And so have we, shaping them in a way as much spiritual as folk. The elaboration of similarities and differences, the effort to disentangle the religious from the ethnic in each instance, could go on endlessly (itself one of our ethnic traits, the love of analysis and argument).

Which brings me to the matter of our style, of that elusive approach to living one finds so widespread among American Ashkenazi Jews. Sometimes you recognize it by a shrug or a gesture, more frequently, a few years back, in one's intonation or turn of phrase. We associate it with that mysterious interpersonal "radar" science tells us cannot exist and is notoriously unreliable but that most Jews still utilize to detect the presence of other Jews—with occasionally striking results. Even the ways Jews try to hide from their Jewishness or shield themselves from detection by other Jews is part of our ethnic heritage. Overeating instead of boozing, an addiction to the verbal, jokes, a sensitivity to changing fashions—who knows how far the modern Jewish style, for all its varieties and personal embellishments, goes? Yet it clearly derives from Jewish group experience and only peripherally from the Jewish religion. Any serious-minded Jew will find it difficult to attach great spiritual significance to Jewish style, yet without it we would lose something precious. It grounds our ethnic life and is therefore part of us in a way it could never be if we were merely a church.

THE CULTURAL IMPERATIVE

This understanding of our group nature owes much to the thought of the great American Jewish philosopher Mordecai Kaplan. He was the first person, who, in the 1920s and 30s, tried to apply to the Jews the insights of the new science called sociology. In place of race and blood he taught American Jews to speak of peoples and their civilizations—what later more commonly came to be called culture. The first thing a sociologist notices about humanity is that it is divided into different groups. This led Kaplan to argue that the Jews are another such natural group and that no supernatural choice was needed to set us apart from other peoples. Just as all other groups developed a way of facing the world and elaborated it into a multi-faceted life-style, so too did the Jews. And since religion was only one part of a people's culture, even if the pivotal part, so the Jewish religion needed to be seen as but one aspect of an entire range of ethnic activities. Much of the revival of Jewish music, art, dance, and other cultural activities among us in recent decades has been due to Kaplan's insistence that we are an ethnic group and need to take up the full gamut of cultural responsibilities which derive from that identity. Kaplan had gotten this idea from the cultural Zionists before him, specifically from Ahad Haam. Yet he must be given special credit for Americanizing their rather narrower, European sense of nationality and for utilizing the insights of Durkheim and some other early sociologists to help Jews gain a rich, full sense of their group nature. This section of the *Centenary Perspective* should then be particularly pleasing to those Reform Jews who have found Mordecai Kaplan a guide to their sense of a modern Judaism. Yet for all Reform Jews it expresses the conviction that Jews are not a church but, odd as this may seem, an ethnic group. Had the document said only this, it would have pleased no one, probably not even the Kaplanians. The statement on ethnicity must be kept in balance with what went before which spoke of the union of peoplehood and faith, and therefore with what follows, a statement of this people's involvement with God.

CHAPTER TEN

The Religious Side of This People

THE JEWISH NATION

The Bible considers the Jews a nation in the same way that the Hivites, the Hittites, the Egyptians, and the Babylonians are nations, yet it makes a major distinction between the children of Jacob—Israel—and them. The other peoples came into being when God dispersed the peoples of the earth into tongues, lands, and nations after they tried to build a tower at Babel which would reach up into the heavens where God resides. Nationhood commonly results, therefore, from human sinfulness and God's punishment. The Jews became a nation in an entirely different way. God came to Abraham and told him that he was to obey God in special ways, as by leaving Ur of the Chaldees and going to a land that God would show him. In return, God would eventually make of his children a great and multitudinous nation.

After three generations the numbers began to grow, and four centuries later a mighty people existed—the Bible counts six hundred thousand. To them, at Sinai, in a mighty act of

fulfillment and new agreement, God gave the
Torah. No other people had anything like it.
No other people was expected to give God the
special obedience and loyalty that the people
Israel now owed God. At the same time, no
other people could hope for the special gifts of
God, such as the Land of Israel, the protection
of God amid the trials of history, or, as it was
eventually understood, the ultimate vindication
of Jewish constancy when the King-Messiah
arrived to rule the world and demonstrated the
truth of the Jewish assertion that their God
was indeed the one Lord of all the universe.

THE CHOSEN-PEOPLE CONCEPT

Until modern times it was quite clear: God
chose the Jews. They were a nation because
God wanted them to be a nation and this was
unlike anything any other people could claim.
Their nationhood was also unique because it
was based on their having the Torah, the God-
ordained laws and teachings by which they
were to guide their national life. I do not see
that one can deny that the Jews were therefore
understood to have a special status in relation
to God, one closer to God than anyone else
had and therefore a better one. This did not
imply that other peoples had no relation to
God or that the Jews therefore deserved privileges in this world. They would indeed get
special rewards in the life of the world to
come, but in this world chosenness was closely

linked with Torah and its commandments and thus implied special standards of obedience.

Modern Jews have found it difficult to affirm the doctrine of the chosen people in the ways their ancestors did. With regard to God, they shy away from ascribing to the Divine such explicit intervention into history. It is one thing to say God's power moves through nature and even makes itself felt in human affairs. It is quite another thing to say, so flatly, "God chose us." Moderns prefer to talk about religious reality from the human side, emphasizing the initiative of people. Religion seems to us as much our work as God's; it seems easier to understand as more human discovery than God's gift. Now, too, as we Jews for the first time see humanity in worldwide perspective, we recognize that most human beings are very much alike. We do not believe that the Jews are as different from all other peoples as previous generations thought, though, with all that, most of us do not think that they are just another culture. Besides, the democratic view of humanity assigns equal status to everyone. For these and other reasons, chosenness seems dangerous or anachronistic or in need of reinterpretation, though some still maintain it is true.

THE MEANING OF CHOSENNESS

The *Centenary Perspective* sidesteps this issue. This is another instance of no single theology satisfying the overwhelming majority of rabbis. Some of them want every vestige of the idea purged from our Judaism. Others use Zangwill's phrase of some decades ago, "a choosing people," which though acknowledging that we have no specially assigned place in the universe says we have distinguished ourselves as a people by our unique effort to live up to our sense of God's will. Some supplement that with the contention that historic peoples, like individuals, have certain talents. The Jews have a genius for responding to God. I once heard George Steiner, the famous British critic, suggest the possibility that perhaps there was something peculiar in the genetic chemistry of Jews, an odd structured DNA and RNA which gave them their special capacities.

Others prefer to emphasize the message rather than the Jews.

Early Reform Jews, basing themselves on the special affinity they felt existed between religious liberalism and Judaism, proclaimed that the Jews have a special mission to humanity: spreading the idea of ethical monotheism. The idea now seems somewhat pretentious and is not often heard. Some rabbis feel these liberal notions of chosenness reduce God to a passive bystander in the affairs of humanity, including the special quality of Jewish life. Believing that God is personally present to people, at least at certain moments, they speak of the Covenant between God and the Jewish people, the sense of mutual agreement which arises from moments of special insight, when people love. There are also those who, despite their appreciation of the human role in religion, simply accept God's greatness as beyond them and therefore reaffirm the traditional teaching that "God chose us from among all peoples and gave us the Torah."

OUR "INVOLVEMENT WITH GOD"

The *Centenary Perspective* covers all such possibilities with the words "involvement with God." It says further that the uniqueness of the Jewish people comes from this involvement. One may understand this in two ways. The more traditional way would be to say that there is something in the content of the involvement with God which makes the Jews unique. It is the Torah or the Covenant or something about the relationship between God and the Jews which distinguishes the Jewish people. The more humanistic way of reading the sentence would be to ascribe uniqueness only to the Jewish historical experience. One might argue that no other ethnic group has ever been so concerned about bringing God into its civilization as has the Jews. There is no claim here that the relationship of the Jews to God is special, for the universal God treats all people alike. Everyone could have done what the Jews did; in fact, they didn't. The uniqueness of the Jews is merely a historical fact, and one can raise no moral objections to that, since all historical experience is unique.

Regardless of which position one takes, Jewish ethnicity, all agree, is uniquely religious. It has to do with God. It has not and does not exist in and of itself. The paragraph rejects the notion that ethnicity alone can ever furnish a satisfactory understanding of our people. It denies the validity of all purely secular inter-pretations of the Jews. Thus for all its previous strong assertion of the significance of Jewish ethnicity, the *Perspective* now equally strongly insists that the Jews and their ethnicity are irredeemably religious.

IMMEDIATE CONSEQUENCES

The *Perspective* adds two further considera-tions. First, the involvement with God is linked to a "resulting perception of the human condi-tion." Relationship with the Divine has immediate consequences for what it is to be a human being. The Jews are not concerned with just worshipping or being in the presence of God. Jewish intimacy with God results in: commandments to follow, a society to build, temptation to confront, sin to atone for, for-giveness to seek, judgment to confront, and hope that the God who we know is real will eventually become a reality in all human life upon the earth. The particular religious experi-ence of the Jews has given them a vision of the universal possibilities of humanity. Some will want to assert that this view of the human condition is itself unique among the religions of the world. Surely the age-old devotion of the Jewish folk in bending its ethnicity to this vision is without parallel among the cultures nations have created.

Jewish faith in God and thus in humanity climaxes in the Jewish messianic hope. The Jews may be a quite particular ethnic group, with all the concrete, historical individuality that goes with peoplehood. Yet Jewish ethnicity is indissolubly joined to Jewish faith which moves on inexorably from God to people to a messianic vision of sin overcome and God's will as the inner law of every human heart. So in its particularity the people Israel reaches out to all humanity. Again the *Perspective* has repeated its familiar theme: the particular and the universal coexist in contemporary Reform Judaism.

CHAPTER ELEVEN

The Perils of Splitting Faith and Folk

POLARIZATION

I must add a personal word to this interpretation of the *Centenary Perspective*'s paragraph on the people of Israel. What emerges here, as does so often in this document, is the problem of finding a proper balance between two commitments which partially conflict. What regularly causes difficulty in Reform Judaism is such devotion to one of the affirmations that the other one is as good as forgotten. Then those who are concerned about the other belief stress it all the more in the hope of counteracting the protagonists of the first belief. Instead of healthy tension, polarization results. One is forced to choose between positions which, isolated from their counterbalancing view, are not what you really believe. The older Reform Judaism occasionally stressed the religious side of being a Jew to such an extent that our peoplehood was almost lost. Today one might call this religion without *Yiddishkeit*. The ethnic factor, understood in their case as the specifically German-Jewish style, was utterly subordinated to the Protestant religious model.

So early Reform Judaism came to seem very much like a church.

Criticism of that adjustment is quite easy in a time when ethnicity is acceptable, perhaps even a positive value. American social moods moving as fast as they have in our time, we cannot assume that change is permanent. Still, from this vantage point one can wish they had been stronger in their affirmation of a distinctive American Jewish community style. Yet it is not clear, particularly when I think back to the early 1930s and the pressures upon us—I was growing up in a medium-sized Midwestern town, Columbus, Ohio—that it would have been very easy for those trying to win a place for the Jews amid the general community to insist on greater Jewish distinctiveness.

Today I occasionally feel that the opposite sort of single-mindedness is becoming a problem. Some Jews are so proud of our new Jewish ethnic self-consciousness that they seem content to forget that we are also a religion. The reasons for such an exaggerated attention to our peoplehood are easy to appreciate. We have real enemies and they threaten us harm, less seriously on the domestic scene where there is more threat than reality, but radically on the international scene where we see the isolation of the State of Israel and continuing pressures upon it. We must be on guard; we know that in an emergency we must depend primarily upon ourselves alone. The needs of the Jewish people then summon us to duty, and no self-respecting Jew will say no to that call. In such a situation it is not difficult to overlook our simultaneous responsibility to God and thus to humanity. Our energy, our money, our concern go overwhelmingly to the State of Israel, with some funds reserved for our struggle against bigotry and anti-Semitism. By contrast, synagogues, Jewish education, and the fostering of Jewish culture make do with what can be spared. The example is somewhat unfair, but I hope it puts our problem of perspective into immediately recognizable terms.

SOURCES OF THE STRUGGLE

This concentration on ethnicity has strong forces behind it. We turn to our immigrant roots out of nostalgia for the warmth and closeness of an earlier day. The great accomplishments of the State of Israel appeal to our need for heroes and our disgust with most governments. Besides, ethnicity, though nice, cannot make many demands upon us. American Jews overwhelmingly resist the implication that rich ethnicity depends on knowing Yiddish or Hebrew. By contrast, Jewish religion means facing the claims of God and the commandments, even if these are understood in a liberal way. Our need to help our people may get us to attend meetings, organize activities, and give money, but that is a much easier kind of authority to deal with.

The ethnicity-religion issue can be more sharply drawn. There are cases in our community today where ethnic concern reaches the level of chauvinism. Some Jews think of general society or world problems only in terms of how they specifically relate to Jewish needs. When we use our community for what it can do for the Jews but refuse to contribute to its welfare, when we are effectively only for ourselves, then something precious in the Jewish balance between duties to self and duties to others has been lost. I am not saying Jews should sacrifice their ethnic rights for the sake of mankind in some gross parody of Christian self-crucifixion. Rather I am deploring a Jewish ethnicity which ignores God and our active responsibility to humanity. I do not deny that there are still sick Jews who wish to be so pure that they cannot abide the taint of selfishness they fear is involved in caring about their own people. Yet I am far more troubled at the moment by the growing number of Jews whose resurgence of Jewish ethnicity means the rest of the world can, as far as they are concerned, go to hell.

THE FLAW IN KAPLAN'S UNDERSTANDING OF GOD

Intellectually, one may find some vague parallel to this problem in a common, thoughtless appropriation of Mordecai Kaplan's theories about Jewish peoplehood. Kaplan, in clarifying the nature of the Jewish group sociologically, argued that the people was the motive force in the creation of Judaism. For Kaplan, God can play no independent role in this process, for Kaplan's God has no independent status. Rather Kaplan sees the religious component of a civilization, as critical as it is, arising from a need of human nature and responding to it in ways appropriate to that social setting. In the hands of people less subtle than Kaplan this can easily become a way of reducing religion to ethnicity. If a people creates its religion and in due course its idea of God, one can legitimately give all one's energy to helping the people live a healthy ethnic existence. When the group is strong enough, it will get around to religion. This theory can easily be appropriated by atheists and agnostics to justify avoiding religious questions while yet claiming to reconstruct Jewish life. I have often met educators and social workers, and to a lesser degree rabbis, who used Kaplan to validate an ethnicity that had as good as given up on Jewish faith.

From my point of view Kaplan must take some responsibility for this, though his own writings treat positively of religiosity as part of Jewish ethnic life and of the sort of God we might today believe in. The problem has to do with what the preceding paragraph in the *Centenary Perspective* called "God's reality." For Kaplan this means the "reality" that human nature—as science, Kaplan thinks, has shown—is involved in a purposive relation with nature. We are full of plans and projects, and thus really trust that our universe is so constructed as to allow us to achieve our goals. We necessarily believe, therefore, that there are real processes in nature which support our hopes for our lives. We base our existence on these natural realities. They are the reality we term *God*. Our God is therefore as real as the reality in nature on which we rely. But God, then, has no independent reality. God is, so to speak, no "thing," no being, no entity in itself. God is only a word we use to describe many discrete natural processes. God's reality therefore cannot ever stand over against us and make independent claims on us, though for Kaplan we should obviously not hope to do what nature cannot support. So weak a sense of God as Kaplan's, I believe, can easily be swallowed up in individual and ethnic human activity. "What supports me is my God" easily becomes "Doing what I want to do is being in touch with God." Or, ethnically, since the people creates its religion and shapes its idea of God, ethnic activity becomes the equivalent of directly religious acts, the familiar problem of why pray rather than study or meet which has dogged Kaplanians for years. Kaplan, in giving us a rich sense of our peoplehood, has extended it to the point of denying the independence and thus the counterbalancing role of God in Jewish existence. Kaplan is no chauvinist, and his own, unexplained sense of moral absolutes, gives him a broad sense of Jewish responsibility. But his humanism is so rigorous that he cannot give us the strong counterfaith in God which sets limits to Jewish self-love and places it in the sanctifying context of universal responsibility.

OUR PARTNERSHIP WITH GOD

The overwhelming majority of Reform Jews acknowledge that they hold a double premise as the foundation of their faith: there is one God for all the world, and their ethnic group, the people Israel, is intimately and inextricably involved with that God. The inevitable result of such a two-part affirmation is that some Reform Jews have always been more concerned with emphasizing the universal, religious side of Reform Judaism, while others have done the same for the ethnic, particular side. This, as well as the staunch insistence on personal autonomy, has engendered much diversity in the Reform movement. The *Centenary Perspective* here points out that these points of view need to be seen as part of a partnership: God with the people of Israel, the people with its God. That will not by any means eliminate the differences of opinion and practice which result from stressing one side of the balance or the other. But it will at least help us develop a sense of what, in all our diversity, we hold in common with regard to religion and ethnicity.

PART IV

Torah

Torah results from the relationship between God and the Jewish people. The records of our earliest confrontations are uniquely important to us. Lawgivers and prophets, historians and poets gave us a heritage whose study is a religious imperative and whose practice is our chief means to holiness. Rabbis and teachers, philosophers and mystics, gifted Jews in every age amplified the Torah tradition. For millennia, the creation of Torah has not ceased and Jewish creativity in our time is adding to the chain of tradition.

From the Centenary Perspective

CHAPTER TWELVE

Reform's Radical Idea: A Dynamic Sense of Torah

THE "PEOPLE OF THE BOOK"

The chief symbol of Judaism is the Torah scroll which proclaims that the one God of all the universe has given instruction to the people joined to God in Covenant. The scroll itself contains only the first five books of the Bible, but upon this rests our entire sacred tradition, the rest of the Bible, the rabbinic literature, and the teaching of Jewish sages to our own time. In a sense, the word *Torah*, comprehensively taken, is synonymous with *Judaism*—and, since the latter term is only a century or so old, may be considered its predecessor. Many religions have sacred books and all have traditions, some book-based and some essentially oral. Judaism is uniquely centered on God's having communicated in words, even in books. Scholars have seen this as the root of the Jewish emphasis on intellect and education. If God has given us a book of divine truth (really a collection of books), only fools would fail to study it with the closest attention. Since interpreting the book and drawing forth its implications for situations unspecified there gained the authority of the text itself, Judaism became a religion heavily based on tradition. Mohammed was so impressed with this conception of religion that he called for Muslims to treat those who were "people of a book" differently from those who were not. One quick way of distinguishing between the general character of Eastern religions and those of the West, Judaism and its daughters, is still this notion of revelation, of God giving the faithful rules for and an understanding of life.

THE DEFINITION OF TORAH

Because *Torah* is a term so rich in meaning to Jews it has resisted translation and made its way into the vocabulary of the most un-Hebraicized modern Jews and of non-Jewish students of Judaism. The common English translation, "law," is wrong and misleading in a way that tends to disparagement. A good deal of the Torah scroll books, for example, is not law, and that certainly holds true of most of the Bible and the midrashic side of rabbinic literature. Law is a central category in Torah, but to equate the two gives rise to attacks on the character and worth of Judaism which go back to the writings of the apostle Paul in the New Testament.

What *law* commonly means to people is a set of rules, detailed, difficult and annoying, by which one is judged and generally pronounced guilty of some infraction or another. Religion, which begins by loving God with all one's heart, soul, and might, ends up as a set of performances to be done, and thus rather dry and mechanical. Anyone who has suffered through hearing Judaism denigrated as an arid legalism will shudder at the implications of translating *Torah* as "law." (Paul may have gotten his distorted view of Torah—as other Christians certainly did—from using the Greek translation of the Bible which renders Torah as *nomos*, "law.")

The Hebrew root of the word Torah is *y-r-h*, whose most concrete usage is for casting something in a certain direction, as in shooting an arrow. More abstractly it comes to mean "to teach," as in the first words students beginning Hebrew learn when they are told to call their teacher *moreh* or *morah*. We should probably translate *Torah* as "The Teaching." While that has some nice religious associations and could include much besides law, it seems far better simply to use the Hebrew term untranslated and thus not lose any of its unique connotations.

A DEVELOPING SENSE OF TORAH

Reform Jews initiated a new movement in Judaism by their new sense of Torah. Biblical Judaism is centered around a decisive act which took place at Mount Sinai. There God fulfilled and completed the Covenant made with Abraham and his descendants, by speaking

directly to the nation derived from the Patriarchs, making ten unparalleled personal utter-
ances, and, when that proved frightening to the
people, giving the rest of the Torah to Moses to
transmit to them. The Bible understands other
prophets to have followed Moses and communicated special aspects of God's will. It also has
poems, proverbs, speeches, and narratives
whose relation to God is not clearly specified
but which are apparently considered to be
derived from God and thus sacred.

By the time of the rabbis the Jewish idea of
revelation is more fully elaborated. God uses a
"holy spirit" with which to inspire some
people to write. The rabbis judged the Song of
Songs to have been written under the influence
of the holy spirit and included it in Sacred
Scripture, but said the Book of Ben Sirach had
not so been written and barred it from the
Bible. More important, the rabbis said that
what Moses had received from God was not
only the Written Torah, the first five books of
the Bible, but the Oral Torah as well. The latter
consisted of relatively independent traditions
concerning Jewish life and values. It also
included the rules for the proper way to interpret the Written Torah or extend the Oral
Torah to meet new conditions of Jewish existence. The rabbis could not conceive of a
conflict between the two kinds of Torah and
considered them only two aspects of one,
complex, consistent, living heritage. As we now

read what the rabbis of the first and second century of the Common Era did to keep Judaism vital, particularly in the wake of the destruction of the Temple, previously the central institution in Jewish religious life, we marvel at their flexibility and ingenuity. Their doctrine of the Oral Torah appears to us an extraordinarily creative way to keep Judaism from becoming chained to a text set down a millenium or so previously. Through the Oral Torah they developed biblical Judaism so as to meet the difficulties and opportunities of a new time. Since these processes of change could be carried out by any generation of learned Jews, Judaism now had a method for meeting the unexpected and staying alive.

STAGNATION OF THE PROCESS

Had the flexibility of these early centuries of rabbinic creativity continued into the modern period, there probably would have been no need for the creation of a Reform movement. In theory, the Oral Torah puts such power into the hands of the rabbis that, using it to a maximum, they could have introduced many of the changes we now take for granted as desirable in a modern Judaism. Many things prevented this from being the case. Rabbinic law works largely in terms of precedent, and by modern times there were so many precedents and such respect for predecessors that it was difficult to authorize modification of traditional practice.

Jews had for centuries lived in segregation and under oppression, making trust in general society and radical accommodation to its mores appear imprudent if not sinful. Besides, the demands being made of Jews to alter their life-style seemed intolerably greater than anything Jews had ever experienced in the past. And the Jewish community had been spiritually exhausted by the strenuous effort to survive the difficult years from 1500 to 1800. So the response of the traditional rabbinate to the possibilities of the new freedom of the early nineteenth century was almost uniformly negative.

Yet everywhere freedom was offered them, Jews moved to accept it and willingly paid its price. If survival as such is a primary Jewish value, one may say that in some measures they acted from Jewish motives—they sought a decent life for themselves and their families. One senses something of this unexpected manifestation of Jewish loyalty in their response to the temptations of society. When it turned out that the cost of full participation was conversion to Christianity, only a minority, though not an inconsiderable one, were willing to change their faith. Imagine their unpleasant choice. They wanted to be modern, yet that seemed to entail being Christian. To be Jewish implied identification with a life-style stubbornly oriented to the ghetto and its relatively medieval culture.

A NEW SENSE OF TORAH

This dilemma was broken by a courageous few—lay people, it should be understood—who insisted, against what their sages said, that it must be possible to be modern and Jewish, to be Jewish in a modern way. If the authorities would not lead the move to such a Judaism, they would create it themselves. Thus Reform Judaism came into being. It was an effort to accept Western society without accepting Christianity, to create a form of Jewish life appropriate to the conditions of Emancipation.

These first-generation lay tinkerers with Jewish form seem to have had little conscious sense that they were breaking with the traditional doctrine of Torah, that the Oral Torah authorized only certain kinds of change and then only when sanctioned by the leading rabbis of the age. I think they reformed Jewish practice in the same intuitive Jewish way that the ghetto dwellers rushed out into general society. They knew, somehow, that it was right for Judaism not to stagnate, that one could change the modes of being a Jew and still remain true to one's Jewishness. I doubt that their sense of what they were doing went much deeper than that. Not until the second generation of Reform Jewish leaders, rabbis versed in Jewish lore, some university-trained, was it possible to state the new sense of Torah which lay behind their innovative continuity. They were not philosophers, so they created no rigorous new concept. Nonetheless, they evolved a way of talking about what they were doing that remains characteristic of most modern Judaism. They said that God's will can be known by people in every age and not merely through the documents and precedents of ages past. In a time of radical transition Jews have a right to act on what they believe God wants of them in their altered situation. Torah can change—if necessary, radically.

Then the Jewish historians came and proved that the content of Torah teaching had indeed been modified over the centuries. The very books of the Torah scroll were themselves seen as the result of human creation moving through a series of four major phases. This dynamic sense of Torah seemed completely confirmed by many cultural developments, including the theory of evolution and the belief in social progress which accompanied the economic growth of the nineteenth century. What happened at Sinai was extraordinary, but only one of a series of historic occurrences continuing into the present. How Jews should serve God could not be restricted to one pattern authorized by one group but had to come more directly from the people itself and accord with what its conscience found appropriate.

MODERN JEWISH APPROACHES

This basic position has undergone much refinement since. (Below we shall explain four modern ways of understanding Torah-revelation.) Despite the elaborations it remains the basis of contemporary Reform Judaism. Somewhat playfully, though provocatively, one may say that it created "Orthodox" Judaism. Before Reform proclaimed a relatively unrestricted right to change Jewish practice, there was hardly any need to defend tradition's theory of authority. But in the face of the Reform challenge a vigorous defense of the classic position had to be made, bringing the traditional doctrine of Torah to self-consciousness and creating "Orthodoxy"—"the right opinion"—in the place of what had heretofore only been traditional Judaism. Other modern Jewish movements derive their special concerns from this issue. Conservative Judaism and Reconstructionism accept the Reform premise that Torah is dynamic. They differ from Reform only in how the flexibility of Torah should be controlled or directed. Reform Jews have come to be resolutely individualistic, arguing that for all the virtues of the tradition and the benefits of scholarly guidance, the individual Jew must be the final arbiter of what is living Torah. Conservative Jews have insisted that change take place slowly, with concern for the bulk of observing Jews and under the guidance of a body of scholars knowledgeable in Torah and committed to using its procedures when instituting new Jewish practices. Reconstructionists, believing that the Jewish people is the creator of Torah—which they equate with Jewish culture—call for some democratic body, representative of loyal Jews, democratically to vote what the standards for contemporary Jewish living should be. One may therefore argue that, intellectually, Conservative and Reconstructionist Judaism are sects of Reform Judaism, for they derive from its fundamental break with Jewish tradition and build on its insistence that Torah can be freshly developed in every age.

THE REFORM POSITION

In the nineteenth century many a traditionalist Jew, Orthodox or proto-Conservative, would have argued that Torah was substantially static and had not developed in response to historic situations. Thus we hear worries in the Midrash how Abraham, though he lived before the revelation at Sinai—of the Oral as well as the Written Torah—could, as Genesis says, think of serving the three men who came to visit him the unkosher combination cheese and meat. Since one God had given one Torah, every great Jew must have known it and little could have altered in it despite time. Today the language of evolution, adaptation, and social responsiveness is simply part of the self-understanding of most Jews, even of modern Orthodox scholars, the first five books of the Bible excepted. As a result, when our committee came to formulate the section of Torah it found itself confronted with very few problems. A century ago—even a couple of generations back—the Reform sense of Torah would evoke polemics and argument. In our time there is virtual Jewish consensus; the acceptance of Reform Jewish teaching has been that complete. The curious consequence of this situation was that, in the draft presented to the Conference in San Francisco, the statement of Torah was only two sentences, namely, "Torah results from meetings between God and the Jewish people. The records of our earliest confrontations are uniquely important to us; yet Torah continues to be created even in our own time." There had been a longer paragraph on Torah in the working draft* mailed to the rabbis in March, but since that version seemed verbose the committee undertook to prune every excess word from it and what we needed to say about Torah was finally contained in those few words. They said that Torah was as much a human creation as it was God-given and thus dynamic in a more-than-traditional sense. They indicated it was essentially a folk, not an individual matter. And while they asserted the unique value of the Bible and, by implication, rabbinic writings, they emphasized that what is created today may also be entitled to the

---

*For a discussion on the procedure and process involved in arriving at the final document, see the Supplement to this volume

dignity and authority of being called Torah. Since by now these Reform Jewish attitudes were widely understood and accepted, the committee thought not much more needed to be said.

When this draft came to the floor of the Conference, objections were voiced to the brevity of this section. Our colleagues did not object to what had been said, and it was not clear that they thought anything truly significant had been omitted. My feeling was that they believed saying so little implied that Torah had accordingly little significance to us. Of course, the opposite is the case. The doctrine of Torah as dynamic determines the unique position of Reform Judaism, and thus anything which seems to make Torah relatively unimportant detracts from the value of Reform Judaism itself.

Another possible misunderstanding the document's brevity might engender was that Reform disparaged the value of tradition, particularly the multifaceted development of Judaism in the postbiblical, premodern period. That, too, contradicts our teaching, for we insist that not just Sinai or the Torah books dominate Jewish thinking, but that Torah is produced in every age. There was no difference in principle here, only one of form. As a result it was agreed that the paragraph on Torah be expanded based on the working draft's longer text and on the discussion by the Conference.

Some additional suggestions were received after the San Francisco meeting, and a draft was submitted to the committee which resulted in the present section on Torah. It specifies some of the various forms in which Torah has been created, connects the possession of Torah with the need to study and to practice, and removes what some saw as an invidious comparison between the Torah created in our time and that of a previous age.

CHAPTER THIRTEEN

How Torah Arises:
Four Modern Views

Reform Judaism transformed the classic Jewish doctrine of Torah by drastically increasing the role people played in its origin. For the Bible, Torah is something God gives, and when Moses or the kings do not know what God wants them to do, they inquire of God quite directly. Some rabbis could even speak of Torah as having existed with God before Creation. The liberal view, by contrast, concentrated on human discovery often to the elimination of any special act of God. This emphasis on the human aspect of Torah is understandable as a response to the historic problem modern Jews faced. They knew Judaism must change if it was to survive. Since the traditional authorities insisted that the Torah system could not make the radical adaptations apparently required by the modern world, the Reformers made them themselves. Human action was the basis of Reform—and, as they saw it, the basis of Judaism's possibility to survive. If they were right, human initiative was a critical element in Torah.

HUMAN INITIATIVE AND TORAH

Two consequences followed from this assumption. First, as the dynamic sense of history grew in the nineteenth century, the Reformers saw human initiative as the motive force in much of the Jewish religion's development. The Jews, like all other people facing new situations or compelling new ideas, humanly made the adjustments that seemed required. Quickly it seemed so obvious to them that Jewish life had always been shaped and reshaped in this way that they did not see how anyone could deny that a substantially independent humanity had created the Torah and its subsequent traditions.

Some qualification is needed here. The Bible and Talmud do not deny the Jews a role in relation to Torah. The Bible pictures them accepting it out of their free will, agreeing to receive and live by the Torah as a matter of positive choice and commitment. For the rabbis, human participation goes even further, though some rabbis emphasize God's dominance in the relationship. Their Judaism focused largely on the Oral Torah with its manifold procedures for developing new laws and values. They stressed the human factor for the power to decide what Torah now said was in their hands. The rabbis' "humanism" is strikingly illustrated in two passages in the Talmud much beloved of liberal preachers. The annual Jewish calendar, specifically the dates of Rosh Hashanah and thus of Yom Kippur, must be fixed by a human court. Thus we are told that when, in one talmudic tale, the angels ask God when the New Year will fall, God says, "Why ask Me? Let us both go down and see what the rabbinic court has determined." The other tradition tells of a Heavenly Voice pronouncing Rabbi Eliezer right though he is the only one disagreeing with the rabbis over the purity status of a certain sort of stove. The rabbis then remind the Heavenly Voice—with a biblical quotation, to be sure—that it is their responsibility, not Heaven's, to rule on what are the authoritative implications of Torah. Later, Elijah meets and tells one of the rabbis that in that hour God laughed and said, "My children have conquered me."

For all the charm and, by some standards, religious audacity of these stories, Jewish tradition basically thought of Torah as God-given and limited the human role in reinterpreting it to the patterns which God has prescribed and the precedents the masters of prior generations had set. Thus the possibility of granting women equal rights to men in Judaism hardly comes within the sphere of human initiative in traditional Jewish law but seems to many of the earliest Reformers exactly the sort of thing they must and should do. To be precise, we should say that there is only a relative difference between the role of people in defining duty in Orthodoxy and Reform, but it is great and radical enough to make for a major new direction in Jewish history.

Liberal Jewish thinkers have proposed a number of theories explaining how Torah arises from among human beings. In such a situation the *Centenary Perspective* avoids endorsing any one view and presents a general statement agreeable to proponents of the various theologies. Thus to say that "Torah results from . . . God and the Jewish people" is, by contrast to the classic "God gave the Torah to the people of Israel," to give the Reform Jewish view. The two partners in Torah are mentioned, but no specific role is assigned each, thus allowing people to utilize whichever liberal understanding of Torah they accept. The committee had a problem, however, in trying to find a suitable neutral word to describe what it was between God and the Jews that engendered Torah. In the working draft the committee vetoed the word *encounters* as seeming to endorse the interpretation of Martin Buber. It then settled on the admittedly clumsy locution *meetings* between God and the Jewish people. That seemed to be open enough for various interpretations yet directed attention to what happened between God and the people rather than to either side of the partnership. But the term *meetings* is rather odd, and at the discussion of the document by the Conference it was suggested and agreed that the term *relationship* be used in its place. When this word had been suggested in our committee discussions, I had thought that it was so closely associated with an existentialist interpretation of Torah that it might seem a one-party usage. I was happy to be proven wrong and to learn here, as in a number of other matters, more of what my colleagues mean by the theological terms they use.

I believe there are four major liberal Jewish theories about the sort of relationship, between God and the people of Israel, which produces Torah. Since accepting one or another of these views—or some combination of them, though this is intellectually incoherent—has important consequences for our understanding of what we should and should not do as Jews, I want, most briefly, to set them out here.

THE POSITION OF HERMANN COHEN

The oldest of these positions, that of Hermann Cohen, is also the most radical; that is, its sense of Jewish duty is more distant from the Jewish tradition than any of the three views outlined below. Hermann Cohen, the dominant German Jewish intellectual in the four decades preceding World War I, was concerned with elucidating the essence of the Torah tradition. Cohen was not a rabbi but a university professor teaching philosophy. Following Kant, he considered it axiomatic that moderns should think for themselves, that nothing outside them, so to speak, had spiritual authority over them. Hence Torah had to come from something within the individual, not be given by an external God, no matter how powerful.

Being a philosopher, Cohen felt people got truth through their reason, and his analysis of human rationality led him to two conclusions important for our discussion. One was the necessity of being ethical. Any thinking person should know the call of duty and seek to respond to it in a rational way. The other conclusion was that every mind needed an idea of God to organize its understanding of the world and humanity properly. The idea of one God gave all other true ideas their ground and unity. Thus this God-idea was the basis of ethics. This ethical monotheism Cohen understood to be the essence of Judaism. We may say, therefore, that for Cohen, Torah comes from people using their minds with proper rationality. This Torah mandates ethical action and clear thinking about God.

Cohen also tried to find a way to encourage Jewish practice and community life. The most he could say for these is that they are often useful in promoting ethics and keeping the idea of ethical monotheism alive. Grossly put, such a theory divides Judaism into ethics and ceremonies, with the former rational and directly related to the idea of God but the latter only possibly useful human resources. Ethics are the essence and ceremonies only a social and historical accretion. For all Cohen's appealing intellectuality and the continuing validity of his ethical emphasis, I find his theory inadequate to the sense of duty I have in relation to nonrational, spiritual obligations like prayer and to nonethical Jewish duties like Zionism or, say, making *havdalah*.

THE POSITION OF LEO BAECK

Cohen had a disciple named Leo Baeck who suggested a revision of Cohen's view to deal with personal spiritual needs. As a device to separate the closely similar views of these thinkers it is useful to remember that while Cohen was a philosopher, Baeck was a rabbi. Baeck could therefore understand that religion (Torah) was more than the mind's thinking and that its duties went beyond ethics. Baeck pointed to human consciousness as the place where belief arises. This can be more than ideas, for though we may be conscious of something in only a vague and formless way, it may still seem true and deeply important to us. When we contemplate creation, for example, we often come to feel ourselves deeply dependent upon nature yet called upon to be creators ourselves. Such consciousness is the basis of the religious life. In recent times this has come to be called religious experience, though often that means only emotionally overwhelming events which, unchecked, could validate the grossest excesses of paganism. In

Judaism, Baeck argued, religious consciousness is always channeled by ethical rationality. Thus, against Cohen, Torah derives from both sides of being human, the feeling and the thinking, and keeps them in proper balance.

For Baeck the Jewish way of life includes not only ideas and ethics but the pious practice which grows out of our response to the mystery we sense around us. While this makes Judaism something very much more recognizably religious than Cohen's ideas, it remains a doctrine of Torah in which the Jewish people and its ethnic life are only of secondary interest. Baeck argued that the Jews had made ethical monotheism so much a part of their folk life over the centuries that they and this notion could no longer be separated. Jews now kept the idea alive and their distinctive practices helped them survive for its sake. But Baeck's Torah makes only ethical monotheism essential. The Jews and their observances are valuable but not necessary, a critical distinction when we ask what we must do.

THE POSITION OF MORDECAI KAPLAN

Where Cohen and Baeck looked to the individual for the creation of Torah, Mordecai Kaplan, the American Jewish thinker who began writing in the 1930s, saw it arising from the Jewish people as a whole. Kaplan argued that science, not abstract philosophy, should teach us about the nature of human affairs.

Building on the early sociologists, particularly Emile Durkheim, Kaplan explained religion as the result of the special feelings aroused by group contagion. It was thus not something God gave but what people felt. Society fostered religion, for religion provided the ultimate authority for society's way of life. Religion should thus be seen as but one more part of a people's culture, though the central part. All peoples have created cultures—Kaplan used the older term *civilization*—and we should now understand Torah as the culture the Jews created. As culture is multifaceted and not merely religious, so should be our contemporary Jewish life. That it is restricted to religion is the root of our ills. Our people, through its culture, needs to be restored to health—"reconstructed," in Kaplan's language.

Kaplan has only one external, absolute standard for a people's creativity: the need to be ethical. For him, ethics are somehow part of nature itself (an assertion that hardly seems scientific). While the Jews cannot now claim that God chose them (tradition) or that their essential idea is better than that of any other people (Cohen-Baeck), they can be proud to be a distinct group, for that is natural. They can also take satisfaction from the way Jews built ethical concerns into their civilization over the centuries. Because of this primary emphasis on peoplehood, Kaplan, as against Cohen and Baeck, makes Jewish folkways a primary ingredient of Torah. Through them Jews will naturally express the universal human urge to self-fulfillment.

I think it is true that many Jews use Judaism in the same way other people live out of the repertoire of acts and values their culture makes available to them. However, that is not the same as saying that Jews must or ought to do so. The key question to me in the restoration of a significant Jewish life is that of authority. Why should I do a Jewish act? Kaplan's Torah says, "Because it is your people's way." But I am not certain that just because my folk once did something or want to do something today, I ought to do it. I am a concerned and involved Jew, but I do not see why I should give my ethnic group the power to override my personal sense of what I should do. Besides, I live, as Kaplan puts it, in two civilizations, the American and the Jewish. I can as easily, probably more easily, express my universal human needs in American ways as in Jewish ones. A doctrine of Torah as little compelling as this one hardly seems to me an adequate basis upon which to rebuild Jewish life.

GOD'S SHARE IN TORAH

The emphasis on the human role in creating Torah, which I suggested above is the key to the liberal religion, is clear in these three thinkers. If anything, people have almost completely displaced God. In Kaplan, God is as good as reduced to a term used to describe our sense of trust that something in the world supports our hopes. For Cohen, God is "only" an idea, but God is a true idea and one that all minds should properly arrive at. Thus the idea of God exercises, so to speak, some independent sway over the individual. Baeck's God is somewhat more compelling than that. For him the mind cannot comprehend God in a concept but reaches out to God through a consciousness of living in mystery. Since we sense that there is something beyond us from which we take our being, God has some commanding power over us. That is as far as these rationalists can go in connecting God with Torah. Mostly it is our creation, and thus, since we make it, it can have only limited authority over us. Only in Rosenzweig and Buber does God's share in creating Torah become great enough to make a qualitative change in our relation to its precepts.

THE POSITIONS OF ROSENZWEIG AND BUBER

Both Franz Rosenzweig and Martin Buber believe God to be independent of us, that is, more than our idea or experience, yet accessible to us. Rosenzweig thinks that the history of philosophy, as contrasted to the reality of human existence, makes it necessary to posit this. Buber says we know God differently than we know things. In the latter case, analysis, objective and empirical proof, perhaps even a definition are important to establishing its reality and nature. Yet even with a person there is another way of getting acquainted, a more important, because truer, one. We establish a relationship and then only do we say we know who that person really is. The same, Buber points out, is true of God. We know God not as we might know a thing—that would necessarily be an idol. But, while it sounds odd, we know God in the same way as we truly get to know persons—and therefore God is just as real, as independent of us, yet as involved with us as is a good friend.

Both Rosenzweig and Buber understand Torah as arising from the relationship between this independent God and the Jewish people, the Covenant. (They do not deny that non-Jews and perhaps even other ethnic groups have had similar experiences, though they consider the consequences in the case of the Jews most singular.) They do not think God gives the Torah in the sense of speaking words or inspiring verbal messages, so they are not Orthodox. Rather they call our attention to the way any serious relationship engenders commandment and responsibility. The best example is love. If you love someone, there are things you feel you must do for them and other things that you may not now do. You don't even have to be told this, but you know yourself that this is required of you. If the relationship is important, you need to live in faithfulness to it and not violate its mutual trust.

Religion is most like a love affair with God, involving all one's heart, and soul, and might. Torah is the Jewish sense of duty and expectation arising from its love affair with God (a rather stormy one, according to the Bible). One might go further and say that the Jews and God got married at Sinai, the first five books of the Bible being their marriage contract, the rest of the Bible being their diary and love letters. All of Jewish life, then, is an effort to live up to the match we were so lucky to make.

Torah in Buber and Rosenzweig's view is created by people, but only in response to a real God who stands over against them. Their Jewish sense of what they know they must do comes from being involved with God, though they work out its details. And because we share our people's historical relationship with God, Torah may start with us individually, but cannot end until it includes our people and a concern for its tradition.

I find Buber's view the most appealing of our modern ideas of Torah and yet not fully satisfactory. It does explain a lot of what I believe. Since Torah here is based on a relationship with God, Buber's view shows why we must give Torah some sway over our lives. Since it understands that Jews are members of an ethnic group and not a church, it knows that the responsibilities of Torah are as much communal as individual. Yet it falters in integrating these two aspects of our being, our personal love of God and our sharing of our people's unique experience of God. Mostly, it tends to put the emphasis on what the individual feels is right, undercutting law and weakening the role of tradition in our lives. For all its sense of God, ethnicity, and revelation, this position does not move on to validate community standards in some fresh liberal way that would be more than ethics and less than Orthodox Halachah.

However, I consider this position more adequate than the others. Cohen, Baeck, and Kaplan have little sense of a real God, and thus verge on humanism, or, in Kaplan's case alone, so exalt the folk as almost to make an idol of ethnicity. My own solution to this problem, theoretical and practical, comes in ending the split between one's self and one's Jewishness. When one is no longer a person who also is a member of the people of Israel but is, at the core of one's being, an integrated Jew-human, then the gap between "what I personally must do" and "what the Jews need to do" falls away. That is not the same thing as saying that God gives us a law that all of us can know objectively. I do not believe God gives or has given such a Torah; I am not Orthodox. I believe Torah arises from the relationship between God and the Jewish people, the

Covenant, and that I and other Jews are the living bearers of that relationship. As we accept the reality of God and identify our inner, personal reality with the Jewish people (by no means, thereby, sacrificing our individuality), we share in the relationship which creates contemporary Torah. If enough Jews lived by their Covenant—that is, with God as part of the people of Israel—common patterns might arise which any Jew would have to take seriously. That would become our humanly created, divinely related, communally oriented Reform version of Jewish discipline, Torah.

CHAPTER FOURTEEN

If Torah Is Human,
How Special Can It Be?

AN ACT OF REVERENCE

When the Bible was God's book and the Oral
Torah had been given by God to Moses on
Mount Sinai, there was no question why one
should give them reverent attention. They were
God's own communications and, in a time
when there no longer was prophecy, the best
way one could be in touch with the Divine.
When Reform Judaism insisted that the various
books of the Torah tradition were largely
human creations, that had the advantage of
allowing unprecedented innovation. It also
devalued the old texts and made them less
sacred.

A simple experience brought the point home
to me tellingly. I was teaching a group together
with Rabbi Norman Frimer, an Orthodox
scholar. After reading a rabbinic passage to the
group he put his book down on a desk, but so
near the edge that it became unbalanced and
fell off. He quickly retrieved it, kissed it, and
put it more carefully on the desk, not stopping
in the development of the theme he was presenting. Kissing books, particularly when they

have fallen, is a nice old Jewish custom which reflects very much more than respect for authors and publishers. It is related to our belief that our books derive ultimately from God—that in loving God one loves God's words, the Oral and the Written Torah. I wonder if liberal Jews with their sense of the humanity of our sacred literature could ever come to such regard for Torah that—leaving aside their sense of propriety—they could ever think of kissing one of its volumes.

CLARIFYING OUR OWN ATTITUDE

This sort of question is most significantly raised with regard to the liberal Jewish attitude toward the Bible. If it is taken as essentially the product of one unusual people in ancient Near Eastern civilization and reflective mainly of that particular social-historical situation, why should modern Jews, living under radically different circumstances, pay very much attention to it? On a simple level the question is liturgical: shall we really read the weekly Torah portions when, say, so much of Leviticus details sacrifices we have not offered in two thousand years and when Numbers transmits long lists and catalogs of no special discernible religious meaning? Or the question may be one of religious obligation: Are we still expected to study the Bible with a constancy and attention greater than we should give to major human writers like Shakespeare, Freud, or our most compelling contemporary teachers?

The problem is reflected, I think, not only in the general Reform neglect of Shabbat and festival morning services (where the Torah is read), but in Reform's indifference to adult Jewish education, personal or institutional. I do not think issuing the *Centenary Perspective* or elucidating its attitude toward Sacred Scripture will change things much. The evil urge being so strong, people who are told Torah is largely human will use that as a reason for paying little heed to it. Yet for Jews prepared to take their Reform Judaism seriously the *Centenary Perspective* says that there is good reason to consider the works of the Torah tradition, though human, different from all other human books we know.

THE BIBLE'S ETHNIC DIMENSION

The *Perspective* says simply, "The records of our earliest confrontations [between God and the Jewish people] are uniquely important to us." Three possible explanations of that last phrase suggest themselves. The first is directly ethnic. If one believes that being a Jew means belonging to a group and participating in its culture, as Mordecai Kaplan does, then nothing can take the place of our people's great, ancient saga. It tells us about our origins. It reflects our values and aspirations. It has been our greatest ethnic treasure. Its contents have kept us unified as a people and alive as human beings. It is no accident that in the State of Israel today, though the overwhelming majority of the citizenry considers itself formally areligious, the Bible is a national passion.

THE BIBLE'S PHILOSOPHICAL DIMENSION

Oddly enough, though from a different premise, the rationalists like Hermann Cohen agree that our special interest in the Bible stems from our being part of the Jewish people. They would glory in the fact that the books of the Bible, specifically the prophets, are humanity's earliest substantial understanding of the concept of ethical monotheism. The prophets not only spoke of it but tried to get the Jewish people to put it into effect in their society, often at great personal risk. We should not only be concerned with the origins of our ideas and be proud of our forebears' accomplishments, but benefit personally from their example. Any thoughtful comparison of the prophets with the Greek philosophers will reveal how much more we remain indebted to Hebraic rather than Hellenic thought.

Yet for all their appreciation of the Bible, I do not find convincing the position of either the rationalists or the ethnicists. As to the rational viewpoint, it is modern philosophy which has clarified and validated the true nature of ethical monotheism. That makes the Bible and other works of Jewish tradition old versions of a truth dimly perceived, hence learned better and more directly from modern writers. They retain antiquarian interest and nostalgic appeal, but that hardly gives them a central role in our lives. Putting the value of the Bible on a purely ethnic level, as Kaplan does, is to raise again the question of ethnicity's commanding power. Or, accepting that, one wonders why less demanding, more rewarding ethnic activities, like folk dancing or fund raising, do not more effectively raise our group consciousness, again relegating the Bible and traditional literature to the status of special or ceremonial concerns.

THE BIBLE'S SPIRITUAL DIMENSION

If one believes, with Leo Baeck, that religion is born in our consciousness of mystery, then one can add a special, qualitative dimension to the ethnic arguments given above. Now the Bible is not just our old basic Jewish Book but one in which much of humanity, certainly the majority of people in the Western world, has come to know what is meant by the presence of God. Our Bible is the supreme document of the dawning consciousness of God around us. Its very humanity, all the personal foibles and personality quirks we see in its pages, makes the spiritual greatness of its authors stand out in greater eminence. Such ordinary people gained so intimate a consciousness of God and set it down in words and images so compelling (for all their difficulty) that we, reading them, are often brought to a deeper, more illuminating sense of the mystery which leads to the Divine. This they linked closely with the need to serve God ethically—the prophetic motif reasserts itself—thus instructing us not to rest content with feeling but to direct this religious sensibility into a life of doing the good. Though some books in other cultures occasionally show this understanding, none brings us so closely in touch with people who sensed the Divine and its commands and wrote of them in ways which enable us to share their experience. Insofar as the rest of the Torah tradition is, so to speak, a commentary on and an extension of the Bible, we must attend to it if we are to know the standard by which our faith and lives ought to be measured.

THE BIBLE AS COVENANT

An even more compelling case for Jewish sacred literature may be made from the Rosenzweig-Buber position, for these thinkers see in it not merely the rise of human religious consciousness, a rather internal matter, but the record of true human relationship with the divine. From our own experience we know that certain events have had a lifelong influence on us and that some things have happened to other people with an intensity we apparently never know. Since Buber and Rosenzweig believe God is real and can be present to people, they can believe that as people met and came to know God some might have found these moments of intense personal relationship deeply affecting. The Bible is important, then, not because it records the first time people ever came into relationship with God; but it is the earliest record which testifies to a continuity of such experience with God and which discloses an unprecedented freshness of contact with God over centuries.

Then, too, the Bible narrates how a people transformed its ethnic existence because it established a relationship with God and undertook to serve God in history. We today who come into personal relationship with God are well schooled in the possibilities of religion (and skepticism), so that we are often screened off from a spontaneous sense of what God means to us or is "saying" to us. We occasionally get the feeling in the Bible or rabbinic literature that we are dealing with slogans or stereotypes. That should not surprise us. It only makes it more astonishing, then, when again and again we are brought into the personal experience of people who have come to know God with powerful immediacy and were decisively shaped by that experience.

If we can read the classic Jewish books staying open for whatever is being said in them, we too may find ourselves repeating the experience of great Jews of other ages, standing before the living God. Is that not what collections of love letters or souvenirs do for us—enable us to relive old, great moments in

our lives? If a relationship with God is fundamental to our personal lives, no book can take
the place of the Bible. If we share the people of
Israel's historic Covenant with God, no other
book can teach us what we have meant and
continue to mean to one another. So, too, the
tradition which derives from the Bible will
speak to us as nothing else in human accomplishment.

"THE RECORDS OF
OUR EARLIEST CONFRONTATIONS"

Whatever our interpretation of Torah, then, the
Centenary Perspective insists the Bible is
"uniquely important to us." I cannot now recall (and my sketchy notes are of no help in
this regard) whether there was ever a conscious
decision made by the drafting committee not
to use the phrase "the Bible" and instead say
"the records of our earliest confrontations." I
think not, and, though it may be an after-the-
fact rationalization, I think our present language is preferable. It allows for some Reform
Jews not finding all of the Bible equally
significant to us. It provides for the possibility
that some archaeologist may find another early
Jewish religious document which our people
will come to venerate. But I am certain that
"the records of our earliest confrontations" is
not meant to be identified with the five books
of the Torah scroll. Rather, the text immediately goes on to join together "lawgivers and

prophets, historians and poets . . . . " No single section of the Bible is being specified as "the earliest," and the term is not meant in strictly historical fashion—the time of the Patriarchs, say—but in the figurative sense of those many, varied experiences which generated the Torah tradition. Whatever the historians or literary critics might understand the earliest historical traditions to be is probably acceptable to us.

Reform Jews will have no hesitation in accepting as "the records of our earliest confrontations with God" sections of the prophetic or historical books. The exact, scholarly decision must be left to the historians and literary critics. We are using the term *earliest* here in a more general way to acknowledge our special attachment to the Bible by contrast to all the later writings created by our people.

TWO DUTIES ARISING FROM TRADITION

Two major duties devolve upon those whose lives are joined to this religious tradition. One is common to all religions, though unusually emphasized here—namely, to live our faith. The Torah is full of commandments and guidance by which Jews are expected to mold their existence. It explicitly says that doing the right acts is the primary means of serving God. Hence to have and value Torah means a commitment to live it. That also stands to reason, for if one had direction from God as to how to live, one ought to follow it, for one could not get help from any better source.

The second duty which comes from having Torah is that of study. The Torah traditions are recorded—recorded, moreover, in language that, with but a little help, almost anyone can understand. Torah study is not by necessity an elitist activity. We are not certain how early there was study of Torah by all the people or how "you shall teach them diligently unto your children" was carried out. The rabbis traced the practice of reading from the Torah scroll in the synagogue (on Mondays, Thursdays, and Saturdays) to Ezra, the Fifth century B.C.E. scribe whose dramatic, public reading of the "book of the Torah of Moses" is described in the book of Nehemiah, chapter 8. That notion does not seem historically implausible. In any case, the regular reading of the sacred texts to the people (the Ezra story repeatedly says that the Levites explained it clearly to the whole community—men, women and children) is something of a religious revolution. When the people know what God has said to them, their priests and teachers no longer have a secret knowledge by which to claim special status or privilege. Any learned person can now discuss what God wants. Instead of hierarchy, a democratic principle rules and its basis is knowledge. The power structure of Jewish communities throughout the ages has been affected by this respect for learning, and thus religious and social factors have created an unusually heavy pressure among Jews for education.

One can also discern an inner impetus to study. The Jewish tradition sees a close link between knowing and doing. One ignorant of the Torah can hardly be expected to fulfill its precepts. As I read the earlier and later books of the Bible I see a shift with regard to motivating people to carry out the law. First one hears much about the rewards and punishments God metes out. In the prophets this not infrequently rises to the level of dire threat. Later a change is felt. I am not suggesting that the belief in God's judgment is given up, only that another way of motivating observance is utilized, namely, educating people. Education then becomes the primary Jewish strategy for getting people to do God's will. The Jewish commitment to study is thus directly related to the religion's major thrust, sanctified living, and so becomes a major religious duty, not a possible option for one's leisure. It is also primarily an adult activity, since the commandments devolve upon them, and only secondarily upon children who study to learn what to do as adults. The whole glorious Jewish tradition of learning thus begins in our sense of Torah. And I would argue that all our modern intellectuality derives from it. As we modernized we became secular. We did not give up our commitment to study. We merely turned away from the old Jewish books to the science and literature of contemporary culture. Giving ourselves to this new "Torah" with the old Jewish motivation produced the unbelievably heavy Jewish contribution to modern intellectual life of which our proportion of Nobel Prize winners is one clear testimony. The content of our study may have changed; our existential sense of what people ought to devote themselves to remains the same.

The rabbis debated whether doing or study has Jewish priority. Since the rabbis were themselves scholars and gained their status by learning, they tended toward the preeminence of study. (Pirke Avot, for example, is full of their exhortations about its value.) But the Torah, which was the focus of their scholarship, itself clearly placed the emphasis on doing. In one popular case a reconciliation was effected between the views of Rabbi Tarphon, who favored doing, and Rabbi Akiba, who favored study. The Talmud records the majority of sages siding with Akiba, but then gives as their reason "because study leads to practice." The *Centenary Perspective* may be said to follow in this rabbinic tradition by putting the two duties side by side when it says of Torah that its "study is a religious imperative and [its] practice is our chief means to holiness."

CHAPTER FIFTEEN

How Broad Is
Our Modern Sense of Torah?

Instead of speaking of the five books of the Torah, the *Centenary Perspective* refers more expansively to the records given us by "lawgivers and prophets, historians and poets." This broader sense of Torah is carried over into the Reform understanding of the tradition which derived from the Torah books proper. Traditional Jews, believing in the Oral Torah as well as the Written, consider rabbinic literature, the Talmud and Midrash and the works which derive from them, as Torah. (By association, the study of such works itself comes to be known as "Torah," perhaps as a shortening of the rabbinic phrase *talmud Torah*, the study of Torah.)

Reform Judaism, focusing on the human element in Torah, can see a spiritual quality in much other Jewish creativity as well. The *Perspective* thus goes beyond "rabbis and teachers" to include, first, "philosophers and mystics." This might be acceptable to traditional Jews, though it does begin to strain the older sense of what constitutes Torah. But the statement then goes on to add a much more inclusive phrase, "gifted Jews in every age." Few limits are placed here on those whom we might see as having "amplified the Torah tradition." Here the Reform attitude is quite explicit. For liberals who define revelation in terms of human discovery, whether it is their music or art, the folk tales they told or the proverbs they coined, the focus on "gifted Jews" is exactly right. They brought their gifts, intellectual and esthetic, personal and ethnic, to the creation of Torah. For those who feel that God as well as people are involved in the creation of Torah, the emphasis will be on "in every age." The relationship between God and this people was not a one-time event, at Mount Sinai, but a continuing one. Gifted Jews have continually arisen over the centuries who expressed the Covenant relationship in Torah forms appropriate to their social context. For both groups Jewish religious teaching is to be found in a far broader range of Jewish experience than rabbinic literature.

IDENTIFYING TORAH WITH ETHICS

The rationalist stream of Reformers, while not limiting Torah to classic Jewish texts, would, however, limit its content, wherever found. To them, only ethics are divine instruction, all other forms of Jewish lore being on a lesser qualitative level. Ethics are true because they are universal, a fundamental characteristic of all rational human beings. Likewise, they are the essence of Judaism. Until recent years the representatives of this view connected it with the idea of human progress. That is, they believed humanity, despite occasional setbacks, shows continual growth in spiritual understanding and ethical accomplishment. Normally, those who come later in a history see reality more clearly, in part because they build on what went before but mainly because history, so to speak, has a way of clarifying the truth. Thus later Jews are really in a better position to say what Torah truly is than were previous generations, a radical reversal of traditional Judaism with its heavy deference to the past and its strong dependence on precedent. Modern Jews, therefore, have a right, even a mandate, to follow their Torah even though it disagrees with that of earlier generations, as the Reform Jews did in their struggle to modernize Judaism. Because many of its adherents took the idea of progress quite literally, this concept went under the name "progressive revelation."

Yet in its prefatory historical paragraph the *Centenary Perspective* said that one of the things Reform Jews have learned in recent decades is that the idea of "inevitable progress" is largely untenable. This section on Torah seems explicitly to reject "progressive revelation" in the strict sense by calling the records of our earliest confrontations "uniquely" important. That implies that nothing since has been as significant, much less better. This does not mean the *Perspective* denies that revelation is continual or that we today are obligated to follow our sense of what God wants of us. The *Perspective* explicitly talks about Torah continuing into our own time and makes this the climax of this section. This rejection of inevitable progress in Torah should also not be taken to imply that Reform Jews should no longer see ethics as the core of Torah. Those who define human spirituality in terms of universal moral obligation will not find their sense of Reform violated by this paragraph on Torah unless they are such rationalists that they do not concede that Jewish "mystics" amplified the Torah tradition. It is not ethics, but steady progress, which no longer seems believable.

GOING BEYOND THE ETHICAL

I do, however, think that most Reform Jews, would no longer want to identify Torah only with ethics. The objection is not to saying that Torah is fundamentally ethical, rather, some have understood that to mean that whatever is not an ethical teaching is not part of what God truly wants of us for all its educational or folk value. Our understanding of Torah has changed because our sense of what it is to be a person and a Jew has changed. A person is at least someone who thinks clearly and does the right, but also very much more than that. When we are most fully human—choosing, loving, willing—it is not merely our minds or consciences that are at work but all of us at

once. That must include, without overempha-
sizing them, our emotions—more, that full
integration of mind and emotion and unfath-
omable individuality we call a self. If we live
out of the mystery that leads to God or out of
a relationship with God it must be with more
than our reason and our ethical sense. God
must be be giving us Torah for the whole person, Torah which is thus more than ethics.

In the same way, a Jew is more than a
rational individual born into this odd ethnic
group. For many of us, Jewishness is no secondary, almost accidental matter but a primary
part of who and what we are. In good measure
we live our individuality as one of the people
of Israel. Hence our Torah must be more than a
universal ethic with an ethnic coloration. It must
be an instruction directed to the sanctification
of the Jewish people as a whole, beginning with
each individual Jew. In this instance it makes no
difference whether we think our people created
culture-Torah or that God and the people create
it out of their relationship. In both cases the
corporate dimension, the particularly Jewish
aspect, is emphasized. As against the older
Reform Judaism's rationalism, so concerned
with individual autonomy and universal ethics,
Reform now sees individuality as having greater
dimension and focuses much of its attention on
Jewish peoplehood. This paragraph on Torah
then reflects the themes which run through
the *Centenary Perspective* as a whole. (These

emphases are basic to section IV, religious duties, discussed below in *Reform Judaism Today: How We Live*, Part II.)

LIMITS TO WHAT IS TORAH

For myself, I find it important to specify certain limits to what should be regarded as Torah. There is a danger in saying that people or the Jewish folk play a major role in creating Torah. One can easily exaggerate that thesis so that almost every personal or Jewish activity is given the high significance of Torah. Perhaps I can best indicate my desire for some restriction of the idea by exaggerating its possible negative consequences. On the individual level, one often hears great people in our time referred to as prophets, and I would agree that one might have heard a transcendent call in some of the addresses of Stephen Wise or Martin Luther King, Jr. This makes us call them modern prophets. But I doubt that their words, or even their deeds, will continue to exalt us for very long. Already their teaching begins to fade and some of it seems quite dated.

I am, of course, suggesting that significant truth has a way of lasting generations or centuries. Much of our Torah tradition has been around for millennia. I do not think I underestimate the value of an utterance which speaks God's word to a given moment, but I feel that a good deal of what passes for great truth in our time, for our equivalent of Torah, is quite fleeting, more a matter of moral fashion than of lasting insight. With our modern temptation to see worth only in the novel, we expect spiritual breakthroughs to come with some degree of regularity. I am saying that not everything that is intriguing should be considered Torah and treated with its appropriate dignity. I think that caution might be uttered by humanist interpreters of Torah. Those of us who take God's role in revelation seriously (though we do not think God says words or dictates details) will regularly want to know, for all the difficulty involved in finding it out, whether we hear God speaking to us, from some contemporary effort. I think I have found my relationship with God stimulated or enriched by some modern writing or painting, for example, and hence my sense of what might be Torah is fairly comprehensive. But trying to attend to God as well as to human creativity, I do not see or hear very much that deserves to be called Torah.

I find the same applies on the folk level. Not every act of ethnic invention is modern Torah. Again let me exaggerate. One of the greatest folk creations of American Judaism, I would contend, is our variety of *oneg shabbat*. The modern use of the term stems from Chaim Nachman Bialik, the great poet and literateur of the early part of this century. He conceived of the idea of having literary afternoons on Shabbat at his Tel Aviv home, thus giving special content to the day's secular observance. The term was taken up in the United States to denote the synagogue activities following the late Friday evening service (themselves an American innovation, attributed to Issac Mayer Wise). Despite the effort to introduce into this period some singing, discussion, or other cultural activity, the American *oneg shabbat* remains mainly a time for eating and drinking—almost universally coffee or tea with cake and cookies, not infrequently those with eastern European Jewish ethnic overtones as transformed by our affluence. Besides eating and drinking, the major activity of our *oneg shabbat* is *schmoosing*—greetings are exchanged, news transmitted, gossip passed, temple and community affairs attended to, all in a happy buzz of in-group familiarity. In the American *oneg shabbat* culture is dispensable, the food and talk are not. It is not what Bialik had in mind, but it meets our situation: in the synagogue, not at a home; in connection with services, not as a secular activity; with devotion to chit-chat, not culture. Yet nowhere in our community does the simple folk nature of the Jew appear as clearly as in this weekly gathering of the clan and renewal of our ethnic ties. By contrast, the service does little for most Jews, either in moving them personally or bonding them to their people. At the *oneg shabbat* they are involved, animated, caring, and ethnic in ways that only rarely have analogues in the sanctuary.

If, then, our people creates Torah, we should have less service and more *oneg shabbat,* for it truly expresses and enhances our peoplehood. Yet the proposal to do away with the service altogether and, after some delay to let us get over dinner, to spend our time together in Jewish talk is too radical, even for humanistic interpreters of Torah. Somehow they know that the Jewish people ought to aspire to more than *schmoos* and that to turn the Sabbath essentially into what the folk most want is wrong. Even for them, I am arguing, modern Torah has to be as much an ideal as what Jews will readily do. For those who think God has a share in Torah it is clear why the *oneg shabbat* cannot replace services, though Jews today prefer talking to one another than to God. Ethnicity without simultaneous devotion to divinity should not be considered Torah. I concede that in Judaism the line between "pure" ethnicity and responsiveness to God is difficult to draw and is probably fictitious. But it is a useful analytic tool in our time when secularity has such a hold on Jews. The emphasis on ethnicity easily becomes an excuse for ignoring God, and we prefer a Torah of folk activities, so we need not attend much to religious obligations. In sum, not everything that passes for *Yiddishkeit* should be part of our sense of Torah.

In our present Jewish mood, I cannot judge whether the danger of equating Torah with tribalism is greater than that of equating it with individual creativity. As with so many of the problems this the *Centenary Perspective* addresses, it is the balance among the beliefs which is critical. Reform Judaism is committed to individualism, peoplehood, and the service of God. Undue emphasis on any one of those beliefs leads to a skewed doctrine of Torah.

"THE CREATION OF TORAH HAS NOT CEASED"

One further theme requires elaboration, though here the century or more of Reform Jewish teaching has been successful enough that it can be put briefly. "The creation of Torah has not ceased and Jewish creativity in our time is adding to the chain of tradition." That has become so much a part of modern Judaism that many an Orthodox spokesman would find the sentence acceptable. The great scholars of our age, they would say, like the great scholars of every age, add to Oral Torah. Yet that was not always so acceptable a belief. For much of the nineteenth century in Europe and in some pockets of world Jewry today, it is unthinkable to call innovations Torah. One great Orthodox figure of the last century, a rigorist to be sure, the *Hatam Sofer* in Hungary, said bluntly, "Anything new is forbidden by the Written Torah." Modern Orthodox leaders and Reform Jews would likely disagree over what is meant by the *Centenary Perspective*'s inclusion in Torah of "Jewish creativity in our time." The

Reform Jewish construction would likely be quite broad indeed, going far beyond the work of Jewish legal authorities to include artistic, cultural, and institutional creations of our people. Even though I have said we need some limits to our liberal reading of what is Torah, we would still see significant religious value in areas which traditional Jews would consider essentially profane.

The *Perspective* does not often resort to traditional terms, for our committee felt people would be more likely to think about what was being said if they heard it in reasonably fresh language. Yet here an old, highly charged phrase is utilized; "the chain of tradition." Though it was limited, to be sure, there was a sense in the classic Jewish understanding of Torah that succeeding generations added to what had gone on before. Reform Jews, for all their broadening of what should be considered Torah, believe they are restating that old Jewish truth. Indeed, they would insist that the dynamic way they conceive of the development of Torah is far truer to what in fact happened than any other interpretation—that, therefore the Reform view of Torah is today the authentic one. It, like other "Jewish creativity in our time," is not a break with the past but the proper continuation of it, and hence another link in "the chain of tradition." And seeing Reform Judaism itself as an extension of the Torah tradition, the *Perspective* uses a traditional phrase to describe its teaching.

SUPPLEMENT

*How a Document
Came to Be Written*

I. THE SITUATION WHICH CALLED FOR THIS STATEMENT

Reform Judaism: A Centenary Perspective was adopted by the Central Conference of American Rabbis at its meeting in San Francisco on June 24, 1976. This was the first time since 1937 that the Conference, the organization of the Reform rabbis of the United States, Canada, and some other countries, had formally articulated its sense of "the spiritual state of Reform Judaism." Since such religious declarations are rather rare, they merit close study, and that is the purpose of this commentary. As chairman of the committee which produced the document and as one who has taught modern Jewish thought to Reform rabbinical students for nearly twenty years, I hope I can add some special insight to those who wish to read this statement with some care. I think it best, as the inclusion of this supplement indicates, to describe the context in which the *Centenary Perspective* came into being. We can divide our consideration between the surface, relatively positive factors which occasioned it and the deeper, relatively negative forces which also were at work (the latter hinted at in the document's phrase "our sense of the unity of our movement today").

A Century of Existence: The Reform movement approached the year 1973 with special anticipation, for it would be the hundredth year since Isaac Mayer Wise founded the Union of American Hebrew Congregations (the "Union") and thus laid the foundation for the other national institutions of American Reform Judaism. Previous attempts to found a rabbinical school in the United States had failed, but once Wise had a group of congregations behind him, support for his Hebrew Union College (the "College"), founded in 1875, was relatively assured. In turn, the graduates of the college provided the basis for the establishment of the Central Conference of American Rabbis in 1889.

In 1973, then, Reform Judaism would celebrate a century of nationally organized existence, itself a good reason for celebration. But the event had more than internal significance. Because of the special characteristics of Jewish history in the United States, Reform Judaism is the oldest nationally organized form of Jewish religious life in this country, and its tripartite structure—congregational, rabbinical, and rabbinical school—has largely become the model for other Jewish religious movements in this country, for their central institutions were founded after those of Reform Judaism. So the centenary of the Union would say a good deal about American Jewry as a whole.

The Work of the Commission: The committees planning the Union's celebration did not want merely to rejoice over past accomplishments, but thought this a good time to look to the future as well. A number of groups of lay people and rabbis was appointed to try to project the directions Reform Judaism should be taking as it moved toward the year 2000. A key consideration was the nature of Reform Jewish belief. A commission of eminent scholars and rabbis with some lay members and a host of consultants was appointed by the Union, the College, and the Conference jointly to prepare a new platform for the movement. Taking its mandate seriously, the commission discovered that the number of problems of great seriousness Reform now faced was overwhelming. Thus at one of its meetings it listed as needing treatment twenty-seven separate themes, such as the nature of God today; who is a Jew?; intermarriage; and biomedical ethics. The commission concluded that the challenges of the time were too great to be met with the sort of short statements ("platforms") which had been issued by a group of Reform rabbis in Pittsburgh in 1885 or by the Conference in Columbus, Ohio, in 1937. Something very much more substantial was required, and some commission members suggested that the sort of small library statements issued by the Second Vatican Council might be an appropriate model. With such a task before it, the commission found its work barely begun by the time of the Union centennial convention in 1973. Unfortunately, the hope that something might be made ready by the time of the College's celebration in 1975 was also frustrated. The commission had by then lost its momentum and seemed, for various reasons, effectively to have ceased operating. (Its records were in due course made available to the Conference committee which wrote the *Centenary Perspective*. They are now available at the American Jewish Archives at the College's Cincinnati campus.)

The Continuing Need: Perhaps the impulse to produce a new statement about Reform Jewish belief might have died then had it not been for a number of other, essentially negative factors that kept the idea alive. Since the late 1960s a number of thoughtful Reform Jews had been concerned that their movement no longer had a clear sense of direction, that it was not responding directly to the challenges posed by our unsettled times. Many people had become skeptical about our heavy reliance on the ideas of Western civilization generally and felt that our religion should now be giving us a more positive sense of human values. They also held the opinion—hardly separately from the previous one—that what had happened to the Jewish people in the past few decades demanded changes in the way we thought of ourselves as Jews and expressed it in our lives. Perhaps individuals had found ways to meet this experience of cultural discontinuity. The movement as a whole had not confronted it. Nearly forty years had passed since the Columbus Platform. This spiritual discontent merited a response.

This mood was exacerbated by a debate on intermarriage which broke out in the Reform rabbinate and threatened to split the movement as a whole into two groups, those championing freedom and those calling for greater adherence to tradition. I have reviewed this controversy in Book I to provide a proper background for understanding the section of the document dealing with Reform Judaism's diversity. Here I think it important to note only that the general concern about the direction of Reform had, through the polarization which developed around the intermarriage issue, been channeled into such antagonistic positions that schism seemed possible. This led Robert Kahn, who devoted most of his *President's Report* to the 1975 meeting of the Conference to the problem of the divisions within Jewry, to approach those in Reform Judaism with the following climactic suggestions:

There is still one more area in which we can find reconciliation. We need, it seems to me, to find a definition of our movement which can pull together its disparate factions. When white light is viewed through a prism, it is broken down into a spectrum of colors. Would it not be possible to bring the prismatic divisions into which the light of Reform has been broken into unity again? This was attempted in Pittsburgh; it was revised in Columbus; perhaps the process should begin again in Cincinnati as we celebrate the one hundredth anniversary of our movement.

I should like to offer, for your thought, the beginnings of such an affirmation of the principles of Reform Judaism.

I.

Reform Judaism is an interpretation of the Jewish faith. We claim the same right of interpretation and re-interpretation which was claimed by the prophets, by the Pharisees, by the Kabbalists, by the Chassidim. We base our interpretation upon a free and non-authoritative exploration of our sacred literature, liturgy and life-story. We are open to the discoveries of modern science. We seek to apply and to live by Judaism's abiding truths in a democratic and pluralistic society.

In so doing, we do not reject any body of Jews (not even those who reject us), but extend to our fellow-Jews of differing interpretation our loving fellowship in the service of our people and our God.

II.

When we say that we believe in God, no matter how we define that term, we affirm the Jewish conviction that the universe makes sense, that this world is not chaos (tohu va-vohu), a blind and purposeless succession of physical-chemical events, but a cosmos, an orderly, intelligible and purposeful process.

Even though we may not be able to grasp that process in its entirety, we are aware of the continual working of a creative power. And even though the order of nature seems impersonal (which accounts for much of human suffering), at the same time we recognize within it a progressive evolution toward ever higher forms of life, reaching their climax in the flowering of human personality.

III.

When we say that human beings are created in the divine image, we affirm the existence within us of spiritual qualities which rise above the natural order; vision, compassion, a sense of the holy, a realization of our infinity and, above all, a knowledge of good and evil, and the freedom to choose between them. In that freedom, human beings can sink to the level of the animal and cause great suffering to their fellows, or rise to their full stature as children of the Eternal.

IV.

When we say that God has given us Torah, we affirm our faith that morality is not the invention of man, but written into the structure of the universe. The apprehension of ethical principles, like the comprehension of physical laws of nature, is a process of progressive revelation in which our people have played a primary role throughout the centuries. In Torah, both the revelation of the eternal moral order which comes down to us from the past, and the word of God still waiting to be heard, we recognize the demand for response by men and women equally to the highest values of Judaism.

V.

When we Reform Jews pray, and when we gather for public worship, we affirm the need of the human soul for spiritual companionship, and the outreach of the heart toward the spiritual power residing in the universe. We look upon the traditional pieties, the order of worship, the holy days and sacred symbols of our tradition as having a myriad meaning and endless possibilities for inspiration, identifying us with our past, uniting us with our people, pointing toward our purpose. As Reform Jews, while not regarding these traditions as binding upon us, we think of them as options and opportunities for the ever-renewed hallowing of our lives.

VI.

When we speak of the mission of Israel, we share the special vision of our ancestors, who conceived of themselves as set apart both by promise and by hope toward the goal of perfecting the world under the kingdom of God. Thus we affirm the meaningfulness of history, not as the endless rise and fall of the tides of power, but the working out of moral truth in the laboratory of space and time. Our survival is testimony to that vision. Our role in history has been multiple; suffering servant, surviving witness, faithful teacher, holy nation, whose constant aim has been the righting of wrong, and bringing ever nearer the Messianic goal of a just and peaceful world.

In the Diaspora, our mission is to share these goals with our neighbors and to work with them toward their fulfillment, as a light unto all peoples.

In Israel, our mission is to help make it possible for those in physical need or spiritual hunger to be gathered into the land, and to aid them in the building of a State in which the principles of Judaism can be applied to every aspect of human life, so that Israel shall be like a pilot light unto the nations.

VII.

We pledge ourselves to the survival of the Jewish

people. We will share the responsibility for that survival with all our hearts, and all our might. We affirm the priority of every Jewish need. In the absence, however, of sufficient human and financial resources to fulfill them all at once, we will seek, by thoughtful and democratic processes, to respond to the most pressing without neglecting the rest.

VIII.

In accordance with our faith in progressive revelation, we affirm the right of Rabbis and congregations to continue the process of interpreting the Jewish faith by the varied responses of intellect, emotion and temperament which characterize all human life, and to continue to search as individuals and as congregations for more light and more love, seeking, not in mutually exclusive nor competitive ways, but with mutual respect, to foster the growing values of our faith.

I present this brief affirmation in the hope that it may help to lead us in binding together the many colors of the Reform spectrum into a single rainbow of promise and of hope.

This was the immediate background for the centenary statement we now have before us.

II. THE COMMITTEE'S SENSE OF ITS TASK

The Committee and Its Members: The members of the Conference agreed with Kahn that "We need . . . to find a definition of our movement which can pull together its disparate factions." They voted that a committee be appointed which, on the basis of his effort, would bring in such a statement for consideration at the Conference's June 1976 meeting. In November, after the Fall Conference Executive Board meeting, the new president, Arthur Lelyveld, appointed an ad hoc President's Message Committee to deal with this matter. It consisted of the following rabbis (school of ordination—C=Cincinnati, NY=New York—and date of ordination in parentheses): Gerald Goldman, Plainfield, N.J. (NY '64), Robert Kahn, Houston, Texas (C '35), Daniel Polish, Washington, D.C. (C '68), Elliot Rosenstock, South Bend, Ind. (C '61), Robert Rothman, Rye, N.Y. (C '57), Samuel Sandmel, Cincinnati, Ohio (C '37), Ronald Sobel, New York, N.Y. (C '62), Jack Stern, Jr., Scarsdale, N.Y. (C'52), Alfred Wolf, Los Angeles, Calif. (C '41), Sheldon Zimmerman, New York, N.Y. (NY '72), and, as chairman, Eugene B. Borowitz, Port Washington, N.Y. (C '48).

The committee met for the first time January 12-14, 1976, but its work had already begun in the preceding weeks. Since its mandate called for it to begin by considering the Kahn statement, this had been sent to the committee members and their reactions requested in writing. These were then circulated for the members' deliberation prior to the meeting. Thus our first session began with a mature discussion of Kahn's "platform." Our work in this respect was greatly facilitated by Kahn's generosity. He opened the meeting by saying that he had thought of his statement primarily as a means of getting this project started. He urged the committee to feel free to follow its own direction, using his words only when they appeared to suit the committee's needs. This was not an empty act, for Kahn never insisted on trying to get his June 1975 version into one or another part of the committee's document but regularly lent his hand to drafts and revisions which went in somewhat different directions (see below). The praise bestowed upon Kahn for this at the June 1976 meeting of the Conference by Alfred Wolf, senior member of the committee present, was thus not the routine fulfillment of an organizational propriety but the honest expression of what our committee felt. To me, Kahn's selflessness in sacrificing his text (as it turned out) for what his colleagues deemed to be more useful set a model for the work of the committee. No one was ever asked to sacrifice his principles, but once we did not confuse ego with conscience it became much easier to work at finding out what people of different views could jointly affirm.

Principles and Procedures: In the account of our work which follows I have divided the general principles our committee established from the procedures it followed. This is somewhat deceptive. In a number of ways the two were intimately joined, and they made sense in terms of one another. Besides, some of our committee guidelines emerged as our work was proceeding, and I may inadvertently give the impression that they were all established at the very first meeting. Despite those difficulties, I believe I can more easily explain what we tried to do if I may separate our aims from our process, and I have therefore organized this narrative accordingly.

I think it also important to note that in much of what follows I have relied upon my memory. The committee did not take minutes of its proceedings, only of the substantive decisions with regard to the text of the document itself. I regret this, since I have only occasionally been able to recall who was responsible for a given interesting idea or valuable phrase, and I wish it were possible to give my colleagues all the credit they deserve. Moreover, the committee felt that our experience together, the give and take of suggestion and rejection, of proposal and its improvement, was uniquely rewarding to us. It would be interesting now to retrace that procedure and relive the emergence of our collective text. But such details are now beyond recall. We were all so intensively involved in the deliberations that none of us wished to withdraw from them to take notes, and we felt we would be inhibited by a tape recorder. Let me therefore apologize here to my colleagues for not giving them, by name and instance, proper recognition for their input to our document. When I am reasonably certain that the committee took formal action on a given matter, I speak, in what follows, of "the committee." When I merely describe what went on or what was involved in a given statement, I am recording what I believe was our consensus, or, to put it differently, this is what remained with me as I recollect the committee's discussions. But each member of the committee may have understood what we were doing in a somewhat different way. Fortunately the reader is now free to reach an independent judgment about this because the members of the committee—themselves writing some months after the document had been accepted—produced a commentary to the *Centenary Perspective*, each one speaking for himself on a given paragraph. This was published by the Conference in the *CCAR Journal*'s spring 1977 issue. Where I believe that what I want to say in these books about the document is quite personal to me and may only incidentally have been in the mind of one or another of the committee members, I use the first person singular.

These qualifications having been stated, I believe it possible to delineate seven concerns which early came to guide the committee in its work. I present them here in something of a logical order and would find it difficult to say at just what point the committee, or I as its executive officer, became conscious of some of them.

The Pressures of Time: First, we were sensitive to the pressure of time. We had been directed to bring in a report by June 1976. Appointed only in November 1975 and meeting for the first time in January 1976, wanting to leave some time for the Conference members to consider our work (see below), we felt caught in quite a squeeze. While the possibility of asking for a year's delay did come up several times, almost all of us believed it would be better to try to get the job done in the time available or, if we could not, report why we found the task set us impractical. As it turned out, by mid-March the response of our colleagues indicated that an acceptable, useful document could be written and that, with some good fortune, the schedule could be met. Yet I think it fair to add that the failure of the Union-College-Conference Platform Commission to produce a document despite several years of work, some professional staff, and a modern budget to work with weighed on the minds of the committee members. People had so long awaited a statement on Reform Judaism that it seemed better not to produce one than to ask for new postponements. Equally, we agreed that it would be better to submit no statement to the Conference than to advance one which met the deadline but did not speak positively to the real situation of contemporary Reform Judaism.

Limitations of Scope and Claim: Second, the committee early recognized that if it was to accomplish anything it would have to be limited in scope and in claim. Again, with the image of the Platform Commission before it, the committee was quite satisfied, as Kahn had been in his document, to produce a statement of limited size. While there are special problems involved in trying to speak briefly about important matters, the committee felt that the only thing it could responsibly undertake was the creation of a relatively short text which it could intensively review and revise. The precedents of Pittsburgh and Columbus gave us some confidence in taking this approach.

Brevity was, however, early linked with the committee's recognition of the special situation in which it had come into being. The previous statements had largely been proclamations of new thrusts for Judaism or Reform Judaism. They spoke for a new consensus which had gathered and which now sought formal articulation. But the committee working in 1976 had been appointed to overcome polarization. Amid the controversy that was troubling our movement, its function was to discover and verbalize whatever significant unity remained. Since its task was somewhat different from that of previous platform writers, and specifically more limited than that of the Platform Commission, the committee agreed, informally, I think, to eschew the term *platform* in referring to its work. It did not want to make too many claims for what it was doing, and it was quite satisfied to let people call its statement whatever they considered appropriate. I endorse that understanding and follow it.

If I may call it that, this humility about our document also arose from a profound respect for the autonomy of the individual members of the Conference. The right to follow one's conscience had been the theological crux of the debate over intermarriage. By extension our committee knew that their colleagues would be outraged if our document made any pretense of setting the standard of what all Reform Jews must now believe. There never was any question of this on the committee. No one suggested that we try to create or consider what we had written a dogma or creed which would supersede the right of individual Reform Jews to think for themselves. Our introduction to our statement makes plain what we consider it to be: "The Central Conference of American Rabbis . . . [describing] the spiritual state of Reform Judaism." We give our "sense"—no more—"of the unity of our movement," not forever, but "today." And this is followed three paragraphs later by an unprecedented discussion of the role of freedom in Reform Judaism.

I think it typical of the document as a whole—and a critical factor in its acceptability to the Conference—that it is scrupulously attentive to individual autonomy. Yet it is also and equally characteristic of it that this concern for freedom is balanced by the limits, small and few though they be, set by our being Reform Jews. And I think that this balancing of freedom with the Reform Jewish claims upon us was an equal factor in the overwhelming support the document received in San Francisco. Again and again in its work the committee dealt with views that had become polarized and needed now to be seen in their proper tension with one another. Restoring the balance of the two poles, without losing their opposition, or, to shift metaphors, hearing the harmony as well as the distinct tones, became the major concern of this document.

For example, though implicit recognition is taken of individual freedom, some demands upon it are also advanced. The organized Reform rabbinate is saying what it thinks Reform Judaism is about today. It does not do so very often. That an overwhelming majority supported this document in this divisive time gives its words special weight. These factors alone should give the individual Reform Jew a good deal to consider while pursuing a personal interpretation of our faith. Should it turn out that our movement as a whole reacts well to the statement and finds it expressive of its present religious condition, that will make the *Centenary Perspective* all the more authoritative, though not giving it an authoritarian claim upon us.

Practically, the committee approached this issue via an intriguing quantitative question. No serious document could gain the unanimous approval of the twelve-hundred-odd listed members of the Conference. The question was then put to the committee: How large a majority would our statement need to win before our committee could feel it had given a sense of "the unity of our movement"? No one would have felt comfortable with a bare majority; few would have been satisfied with the support of two-thirds of the Conference members, as difficult as that is to achieve on controversial matters. Yet the more we discussed this issue the more it seemed evident to us that the extremists of either the freedom or the tradition camp were a relatively small percentage of the Conference. For all the polarization of our membership, we believed that a very large proportion of our colleagues affirmed something of their opponents' position while vigorously upholding their own. Making playful estimates on the first day of our January meeting, we reached a consensus that perhaps 5 or 7 percent of the Conference at either pole of the debate might be so fanatic about their view that they could not accommodate it in any significant way to that of their opponents. If so, then there was a chance that while we might not be able to speak for 90 percent of the Conference, then we might do so for 85 percent of our colleagues. The possibility that there might be that much agreement in the Conference was startling. For safety's sake we agreed, since we still considered it a utopian goal, to adopt an unofficial criterion of 80 percent of the Conference as the group whose views we would seek to articulate. Thus it was our rule of thumb that anything we felt more than 20 percent of the Conference might disagree with could not be included in the document. (The two substantive miscalculations the committee made in using this standard are discussed in Book III. I believe it was Ronald Sobel who, at this discussion, raised the possibility (perhaps as devil's advocate) of our not producing any document, as we could not speak for any sizeable group of rabbis. But the 80 percent figure seemed a worthy goal for us to strive for, and he then enthusiastically joined in our effort to see what we might accomplish in terms of it. Though 80 percent is an extraordinary majority in most democractic bodies, 20 percent is a sizeable minority. We were conscious of whom we might not be speaking for and made every effort to try to find space for them within what we felt we had to say for our majority. We therefore made an effort to avoid overstatement.

To round out this numerical discussion, let me record here that the final vote on our statement at the 1976 San Francisco meeting of the Conference, while not numerically tallied, supported it in overwhelming numbers. Some of those who voted against it did so because they felt that there had not been sufficient discussion, not because they had some major substantive objection to it. In any case, a number of observers judged—the committee members not being objective in this matter!— that there was at least a 4-to-1 majority in favor, the 80 percent or more which all along had been the committee's goal.

Seeking a Strong Statement: The third concern of the committee was to produce as strong and positive a statement as would gain the 80 percent majority we sought. Obviously the danger of trying to speak for so many people was that, in the effort to offend no one, the resulting statement would be bland to the point of being contentless. Some thoughtful critics of the working draft (the version sent to the Conference in early March 1976, on which see below) felt that it was just that. Bernard Bamberger, a past president of the Conference and a much-respected scholar and thinker, found the document so empty that he suggested that we withdraw it from consideration. Alan Sokobin, of Toledo, Ohio, gave a strong indictment of the document for failing to give us new directions for the future, and while he said he would not vote against it, he considered the adoption of so innocuous a statement of little significance to our movement. The committee considered their criticism and that of others at its April meeting in terms of the widespread positive response to its draft and on the basis of its own, admittedly subjective, evaluation of what it had accomplished. It felt its document needed refinement and editing by a competent stylist, but it did not think it should withdraw the statement or that it could make it any stronger within the situation in which it was operating. Whether that judgment was correct perhaps some future historian will clarify for us, but we should be able to see in the next few years whether our statement has had any significant effect upon the Reform movement.

Dealing with Major Problems: Fourth, though seeking to speak as strongly as possible, the committee was determined to try to face directly the major problems of Reform Judaism. These, it was quickly agreed, were the nature and extent of Reform religious observance, our relation to the State of Israel, and how we are to balance our duties to our people and to humanity. Two more problems were then suggested and became part of the committee's working agenda: how to live with diversity in the Reform movement and how to find hope in a world largely despairing and cynical. This decision to face the controversial issues head on marks the major difference between the committee document and Kahn's original proposal. He had felt that division could be overcome by calling attention to those matters where there was no serious difference of opinion. The committee believed that the cause of unity would better be served by showing where, in the areas of our deepest division, we still had major agreement among us. This approach, we thought, should also help us avoid the problem of saying nothing or of restating the obvious.

Seeing with a Century's Perspective: Fifth, though the problems were to be the major focus of the document, the specific occasion which brought our statement into being was the centenaries of our national organizations. Our document therefore had to have a historical base, and while one might just as well ask in one's ninety-ninth or hundred-and-first year just where one had come, the achievement of a centennial seemed a particularly appropriate time for such a glance backward. We were unanimous that this should include not only a section on what Reform Judaism had given all modern Jews but also one on what it had itself learned with the passage of time. Ironically enough, it was not the notion that Reform Jews had been required to change some of their old ideas that stirred some dissatisfaction with the document but the apparent self-glorification some readers found in the description of Reform as a teacher of contemporary Jewry.

Stating Theological Positions: The committee also had some discussion over whether it should include paragraphs on the basic Jewish beliefs, that is, on God, the people of Israel, and Torah. I confess it was I who urged the committee to consider leaving out sections on these topics. By omitting all statements on these beliefs I thought we might show that we did not think anyone could say very much about them in a few sentences. My hope was that people would then realize that if they did not want to consider these matters with some seriousness they should not claim to know what these matters involved. My colleagues, to a man, were opposed to my stand on pragmatic and substantive grounds. To leave these matters out of the document would not motivate deeper search, they suggested, but make it appear to our people that these matters were irrelevant or marginal to Reform Judaism. The document was supposed to serve as a starting point for an understanding of Reform Judaism today, and it therefore required some statement concerning our fundamental theological affirmations. Besides, while not much can be said in a few sentences, some fundamental directions can be indicated, and, considering the low state of belief and affirmation in our time, even to provide this stimulus to further search would be to make a contribution to the education of our people. I was persuaded by the committee and, in retrospect, think they were correct.

However, I know that I am largely influenced in that judgment by the fact that the committee has gone on to supplement the document with its own commentary, and I have in these pages taken the opportunity to suggest further intellectual directions inherent in our few words.

A Concern with Our Own Procedure: Seventh and finally. I had felt from the moment the possibility of my being appointed chairman of this committee was discussed with me that whatever success the committee might have in its efforts would be directly linked to its exemplifying in operation what it wrote on paper. Since we were going to tell others how to live in unity despite intellectual diversity, the committee itself ought to show how this is done. Thus, I had suggested—to already equally determined hearers—that such a committee represent our Conference's religious variety, our geographical spread, and our different age groups. As the list above indicates, this was done and, quite appropriately, without any consultation with me. For my part, I tried to clarify early to the committee, by action rather than by word, that we would operate with scrupulous concern for democracy. Thus before our first meeting I made special efforts to get responses to the Kahn document from all the committee members and circulated them as received. It was a minor matter, to be

sure, but it was an early indication that the
chairman did not intend to dominate the committee or to screen what came before it. I
wanted complete openness to all views and
serious attention to their substance to be the
hallmark of the committee's deliberations. All
members, whether in attendance at meetings or
not, received all documents. On several occasions the work of the committee was delayed,
despite the tight schedule, so that we might
have the benefit of the input of members who
had been unable to reach a decision or to
submit it to us. The committee members appre-
ciated this attitude and responded by applying
it to our relationship to the Conference as a
whole. They happily accepted my suggestion
that we not carry our work through to completion but submit a working draft, though a
responsible one, to the members of the Conference. Quite early, then, they could tell us
whether we were moving in the direction they
desired and what changes of course seemed
appropriate to them. They received the draft in
early March, and when we met in early April
we studied all the substantive changes submitted about which more than a single colleague
was concerned. We did so in the language of
those who submitted the suggestions but
without the committee knowing who had
offered it. We thus exposed ourselves as fully as
we could to the diversity in our midst and out
of it, while respecting our differences, sought

to make as strong a statement as possible of our unity. Having already touched on the description of the process we went through, let me turn directly to it.

III. HOW DO DIVIDED LIBERALS CREATE A POLICY DOCUMENT?

What follows is an account of the steps we went through in creating the *Centenary Perspective*. Reading it, I think, will be as dull as going through it often was tedious, frustrating, and demanding. I shall not at all feel bad if readers who are interested in the content of the document choose to skim or skip this section, and for this reason it has been presented as a supplement to the work as a whole. Yet the commitment to democracy means nothing if it is not worked out detail by detail. Since much of what is said later about living with diversity is to be seen in the actual work of the committee, it deserves recording here. I only regret that I cannot fully convey the tone of what we did. It was carried on wholeheartedly, by people who believed in what we were doing and the way we were doing it, even if that should not have yielded a proposed document or a document the Conference would endorse. I am certain that commitment to the task and to our colleagues had something to do with the unusually positive reception of our work.

The First Communiqué: The committee was formally appointed in November 1975. A first letter asking members of the committee to indicate which dates in late December or January they had available for a meeting, and requesting responses to the Kahn document to circulate before that first meeting, went out in late November. Some weeks later it became clear, from the lack of replies, that something had gone wrong. On checking it was discovered that the list of committee members in the Conference office was incorrect. Additional letters were mailed and the late December meeting dates withdrawn from consideration. To determine a date for the committee meeting, calls had to be made to various committee members, and this made it possible to put some pressure on the committee for written responses to the Kahn document.

The First Meeting: The first meeting of the committee was January 12-14, 1976, copies of the responses to the Kahn document having been mailed in advance. The meetings were held at the College building in New York, Monday afternoon and evening, Tuesday morning and afternoon, Wednesday morning and afternoon. In attendance at most of the sessions, variously, were Goldman, Kahn, Polish, Rosenstock, Sobel, Stern, and the chairman. By Monday evening many of the general issues discussed in the previous section of this account had been decided upon, and the committee proceeded to the discussion of what should be included in each section. Notes were taken by the chairman as well as others on what we agreed should be treated in them. Eventually each theme to be treated in the document received such detailed consideration. Already on Monday night several people (I specifically remember Kahn and Sobel being involved) were asked to report the following morning with quick drafts of various sections, occasionally several drafts being requested for a given topic. Though everyone did drafts and revisions as we worked along, the main responsibility for initial versions eventually fell to the chairman and most of the bulk of the original draft completed by the committee at this meeting was from his hand. The committee turned to reviewing the drafts only after it had discussed its intentions for each section of the entire document. It did so by subjecting the draft or drafts to meticulous, word-by-word scrutiny. There were additions, deletions, substitutions, wholesale revisions, and demands for substantial recasting. The committee was somewhat content to do a rough job at this point because the process went very much better than anyone had anticipated and because it was clear there would be further circulation and discussion of what was done before even a working draft was approved for release to the Conference. The meeting ended with a docu-

ment, substantially in the same general shape
of the eventual one, except that the final paragraph had not been completed and the chairman was instructed to prepare this in accord
with the will of the committee.

This rough draft was sent to all the members
of the committee on January 22 asking for
responses and reworkings. It had been hoped
that much of our revising might proceed via a
telephone conference call of the entire committee. The many revisions suggested made that
impractical. In addition, one of the members
who had been unable to attend the meeting but
wanted to respond to the rough document was
prevented from doing so beyond the deadline
set. Finally, on February 20, three complete
reworkings of the document plus a composite
of four sets of emendations were submitted to
the members of the committee to be considered at a meeting on February 26. Before that
meeting the material of the tardy member was
received, and it became another document
before the revision session.

The Second Working Session: The second
thoughts of the committee, both those who
had been present and those who had only seen
the resulting rough draft, were essentially linguistic. That is, there were many opinions as to
how matters might best be expressed and some
difference of opinion as to what should be
stressed. Yet the revision meeting of February

26 could be entered with the feeling that the committee itself felt it was on the right track. Despite their diversity, none of the committee members had taken strong objection to any topic that had been treated or to any significant opinion in the document. No one seemed to feel that some major topic had been left out or that any essential aspect relative to a given theme had been omitted. The February 26 meeting therefore was devoted essentially to literary revisions of the rough text. Rosenstock, Sobel, Stern, and Zimmerman as well as the chairman were present at Temple Emanu El in New York for this session. In one grueling day a word-by-word revision of the rough document was completed. Since five did not constitute a majority of the committee, the new document was then circulated to all the members to see if what had been produced was objected to by any substantial minority of the committee. The committee's goal at this stage was to produce a responsible working draft which could be mailed in early March to the members of the Conference. Then, on April 7 and 8 the committee was to meet to review their response and, if possible, produce a final version to be submitted to the Conference. There were no objections by the members of the committee to the working draft completed on February 26 being sent to the Conference members for their suggestions. The Conference office mailed it to them, with a covering letter

introducing the document (the committee had also discussed its contents) and soliciting their response by March 31. (The Conference office, normally quite efficient, had inadvertently dropped the section on "The People Israel" from the working draft our committee had submitted to it. As a result, it sent a second mailing, March 16, to the members of the Conference with the missing paragraph.) In addition, each member of our committee was asked to discuss the working draft with at least one colleague and also with various lay people so as to be able to bring to the April 7 meeting a personal report on the draft's merits and failings.

A Telephone Survey: Impersonal mail solicitations of responses from a large group generally draw few answers. Since I felt that it was important to have a good sample of the reactions of the Conference and also to find out from people what they felt about the document but might not want to put on paper, I asked the Conference to authorize me to make a phone survey. They provided me with a list of approximately every twentieth name on the Conference membership list and defrayed the expenses of my calls. I also contacted every past president of the Conference. The calls were invaluable in giving me a feel of the range of response the document was receiving. In all I phoned or was in personal contact with sixty-five colleagues, including Richard Hirsch who phoned me from Jerusalem when the mail response from our Israeli colleagues (which I had particularly written to request) was, for various reasons, going to be delayed. I also received one hundred eighty-seven letters in answer to our Conference mailing, some because I had called the person who had at that time not yet responded to the document. (Another twenty-one arrived after our deadline but before our meeting, and additional mail continued to arrive until shortly before the San Francisco meeting.) We thus came to the April 7 meeting with good feedback. In addition, since the completion of the working draft, I had studied it one Shabbat afternoon with the Board of Trustees of Shaare Emeth Congregation, St. Louis, a class of the Hebrew Union College School of Education, and the Executive Board of the Central Conference itself. This enabled me and a number of other members of the committee to deal with suggestions for the revision of the working draft in terms of some personal experience with it as well as with the written responses.

The Third Meeting: The April 7-8 meeting began with a discussion of some general questions I thought the responses had raised, and these were sent to the committee members so they could give them thought prior to our sessions. In addition, wherever there were several substantive objections to our text, these were photocopied, identified only by number, and collated by theme so that on the master sheets provided the committee could at once see the range of response to a given topic in the language of the person making it.

The major decision of the April meeting may well have been that none of us was to serve as the committee's ultimate authority on matters of English style or usage. We agreed to turn over all such questions to a writer of established reputation whose work on the text would be subject to the guidance of the chairman and review by mail to the committee. This was our response to the large number of complaints by our colleagues—with which we often agreed—that much in the working draft was clumsy, imprecise, and repetitious and that the whole was too long. With the literary questions assigned to an outside expert the committee spent its time on substantive issues. Though there were many suggestions for change here and there, there was a general acceptance of the document by our colleagues that was astonishing to us. There was no substantial outcry against its treatment of freedom or tradition. A number of people considered significant partisans of the antagonistic groups wrote that they found the document at least acceptable and, in some cases, even nicely expressive of their views. There was no complaint that an important topic had been left out (at San

Francisco the lack of direct treatment of social action was mentioned) or included which did violence to a sizeable group in the Conference. The document's structure, specific themes, and overall tone seemed acceptable to most of the respondents, even though they suggested changes for one spot or another. Far more expressions of enthusiasm than of dislike for the document were received. The committee was thus in the happy position of dealing with specific suggestions for change within a framework of a broad-scale acceptance of what they had written. Aside from altering or reaffirming the text in a number of specific instances, the committee decided to explain the statement's purposes by a brief introduction; to have an additional opening sentence about the relation of Reform Judaism to North American democracy; to provide rubrics at the sides of each section; and to give the document the title *Reform Judaism: A Centenary Perspective*.

Present at this session were Goldman, Kahn, Polish, Rosenstock, Sobel, Stern, Wolf, Zimmerman, and the chairman. The resulting text, which was to be submitted to a writer for styling, was then mailed to all members.

Guidance in Style and Usage: Hugh Nissenson, the short story writer and novelist, was good enough to lend his talents to the Conference for the rather unpleasant chore of reviewing and revising a draft which had resulted from these many hands, opinions, and previous revisions. In going over his recommendations with him, I found him to be supremely sensitive to our intentions as well as to the English in which we might best express them. I was not always able to accept his suggestions, as occasionally a given wording seemed required by a committee decision and he and I could find no reasonable substitute for them. On May 10 the Nissenson revision, a much-pruned-and-polished version of our April 8 revision, was circulated to the members of the committee.

While awaiting their responses, due May 25, I had the pleasure of being invited to discuss the April 8 draft with the members of the Union Board of Trustees. It was a most enlightening and enjoyable occasion. That session, as well as a discussion with a class of students in the rabbinical school of the HUC-JIR in New York, indicated to me that the price of our brevity was that even informed readers missed much of what we had condensed into a few words. My concern with our need to follow up this document with additional educational resources may, I think, be traced to these experiences—and my discussions of the statement with groups since it was given its final form has confirmed that impression.

Several committee members suggested some changes in the Nissenson revision, and since these involved only a return to our April 8 version they were acceptable without complete committee consideration. As a result, the altered, Nissenson revision was mailed by the Conference office to all members some weeks in advance of the June meeting in San Francisco.

Prior to the Conference meeting I received a request from some of our Israeli colleagues that a slight change in wording be introduced into our sentence on Jewish survival and that a sentence on *aliyah*, immigration, be added to the section on the State of Israel. I circulated their letter to the members of the committee present in San Francisco, indicating that I thought the former matter was within the committee's intentions. The *aliyah* question had already been posed at the April 8 meeting and the committee felt that 80 percent of the Conference would not support it, so it had not included such a sentence. Believing we should honor the request of the Israeli colleagues, I put it before the Conference, where it was overwhelmingly accepted. (Further details are given in *Reform Judaism Today: How We Live.*)

Presenting the Document: The *Centenary Perspective* came before the Conference late Thursday morning, June 24. It was a somewhat uncomfortable situation for the discussion of a statement of principle proposed by a committee which had been deeply concerned about democratic procedure. Thursday was the last day of the Conference which was to continue only through the afternoon. But, as often happens, the business of the Conference on previous days had begun to back up and, as the Conference had put an overabundance of rich programs on its schedule, there was too much for the organization to do that day and too little time to do it. The members, to whom this had happened before, were relatively tolerant of the situation, though there were occasional ripples of annoyance in the assembled group. Unfortunately, too, we had lost the use of the ballroom where our previous sessions had been held and were now rather cramped in a somewhat smaller hall. Add to this the fact that the best nonstop flight to New York was due to leave early in the afternoon and that a number of the East Coast colleagues were straining to make it and one gets something of the mood in which the discussion of the document began.

Robert Kahn first indicated how the document came to be and moved its acceptance. Alfred Wolf then discussed the process by which it had been produced and seconded the motion. As chairman, I then indicated some of the major concerns we had in mind writing it. We were quite brief, perhaps ten minutes for the three of us. I had thought that there was a relatively good mood about the document from all the feedback we had received. I was not prepared for the immediate will of the body to adopt it and get on to the next item of business. No sooner had our opening statements been made and the question of the *aliyah* sentence put to the Conference then a motion was made to end discussion and proceed to a vote. A standing tally indicated that while the two-thirds vote necessary to end discussion had not been attained, a large number approved of the document and were ready, apparently, to vote for it. (If I recall correctly, the CCAR transcript of the proceedings giving no tally, there were about one hundred twenty rabbis favoring an end to discussion and seventy-odd for keeping it open. Apparently some 60 percent of the membership were already in favor of the document.

The Conference Discussion: The discussion which then ensued first centered around our proposed statement on Torah which, in the Nissenson version, had been cut to two sentences. The Conference objected to this more as a matter of emphasis than of doctrine and suggested that this section be amplified. Since in the working draft it had been much longer, the chairman accepted the suggestion and it was agreed that he would expand this paragraph on the basis of the Conference discussion. A motion to remove the word *mystery* in the paragraph on God and substitute *reality* was roundly defeated. Some questions of wording, of the emphasis on social justice in the document, and on the adequacy of the Conference's discussion then ensued. On several occasions the chairman indicated that suggestions for improving the language would gladly be received for some weeks yet. Another motion to end discussion was then easily carried and after some parliamentary jousting the matter was put to the Conference for a vote. President Lelyveld then said, "The document *Reform Judaism; A Centenary Perspective* is overwhelmingly approved by this body." There was loud applause from the floor and Bob Kahn and I and then Alfred Wolf and I spontaneously embraced one another at this extraordinary outcome to an enterprise we had all entered with such doubt and hesitation some six months or so previously.

In retrospect it is easy for me to say that I wish there had been more time for discussion so that no colleague would have left the meeting with a sense that he had been denied a proper chance to discuss this document. Nonetheless, I know that no major statement has ever come before the Conference with as much prior involvement of the membership as did this one. Moreover, for whatever such a statistic is worth, we had received more comments on the document in the course of its composition than there were rabbis sitting in the room at the time it was voted on. I would have preferred that the acceptance of the document be as free and as participatory as the process which brought it into being. But considering the realities in which we must operate, I believe that whatever failings there may have been in connection with its final acceptance, the will of the overwhelming majority of members was done.

Completing the Task: The committee may have accomplished its goal, but it had not yet finished its task. On the basis of the suggestions made at the Conference meeting and some that were sent me later, I suggested to the committee by mail that five changes be made in the document, ranging from two that were largely verbal to the requested reworking of the paragraph on Torah. This was sent to the committee on July 13 asking for a response by August 13. A number of the members of the committee replied, and some further changes were made in accord with their suggestions. The final version was then prepared, the original of which was sent to the Conference office and a copy to each member of the committee.

Technically that might have finished the committee's assignment, but the various sessions I had conducted based on the document had indicated to me that it could benefit with a commentary. I therefore suggested to the Conference leadership that I would be willing to do such a volume if the Conference was interested in its publication. The Executive Board of the Conference suggested instead that we utilize a series of articles to appear periodically in the

CCAR Journal for some such project. Since that seemed not to supply the space for the substantial treatment I thought the document required, I suggested to Bernard Martin, editor of the *CCAR Journal*, that our committee might produce a commentary to the *Centenary Perspective* for one of its issues. He made some helpful suggestions as to how this best might be carried out, and the result may be seen in the spring 1977 issue of the *Journal*. I was particularly pleased that each member of the committee had a chance there to show how he reads a section of our statement. Obviously, each rabbi approaches Judaism with special concerns of his own, and this comes through clearly in their comments. Yet it was out of such a combination of different approaches that the *Centenary Perspective* came into being. I hope that people reading their interpretations will not only learn something directly from them but will come away from the variety of interests represented with a fresh sense of the unity in diversity which the document calls "the hallmark of Reform."

The committee's commentary should encourage people to study the *Centenary Perspective* to see what it says to them. Only when Reform Jews have had a chance to consider its contents in such depth will we know how useful our committee effort has been. If the document turns out only to have stated what tied us together in 1976, a time of great disunity in our movement, that already will have been an accomplishment. But I believe that what we said went far beyond the understanding most Reform Jews had of their movement and its message. When one sees what is hidden in the few pages of our statement, the things left unsaid, the choices made, and the alternatives rejected, when one recognizes where ambiguity has consciously been resorted to and what content might fill it in, when one sees the ways in which polar faiths have been balanced one against the other, when one recognizes the many strong positive assertions of faith contained here, one comes away with a fresh sense of the power and majesty of the Reform approach to Judaism. At least I do, and that is why, so to speak as a continuation of my work for the committee, I have set down here something of what I see in this document.

My Own Commentary: I have offered at length my views on the *Perspective* because by profession and position I feel I am in a unique position to open up what the document contains. For nearly two decades now I have had the privilege of teaching rabbinical students, and for most of that time I have been writing in the field of modern Jewish thought. I have lived professionally and personally for a long time with the questions raised in this document. I have written my commentary not as an academic exercise but as one of explanation.

However, had I not been a specialist in theology, much that I have strenuously labored to make plain in these pages would not have occurred to me. And I have lived with this document more closely than anyone else. I nursed it through every stage of its long and difficult development; I have been over every one of its words many times with many people under many circumstances. I never had any illusion about its being "my" document, for I know that it does not express my personal understanding of Judaism. It is the Conference's statement, and to that extent Reform Judaism's. It is the document of my movement and I respect it as such. It is the work of a committee I headed and I am proud of it. I hope that by opening up its layers of meaning I may help others catch something of the greatness I see in the Reform movement and the riches I believe are contained in the Conference's centenary statement. Regardless of my official positions, then, I know I speak in these pages only for myself, and yet in doing so I hope I articulate the contemporary spirit of Reform Judaism as a whole.